## What Folks Are Saying About

# APPARENT FAITH

"Karl Forehand is a pastor and seeker who has been on a profound spiritual journey—a journey that led him away from narrow, judgmental fundamentalism into the deep, gracious richness of the kingdom of Christ. I call this the water to wine journey. Karl's journey has not been without pain, but it has been beautiful. In *Apparent Faith*, Karl tells his deeply personal story of seeking and finding the pearl of great price. I am sure this poignant book will resonate with many readers."

**—BRIAN ZAHND, LEAD PASTOR OF WORD OF LIFE CHURCH IN ST. JOSEPH, MISSOURI AND AUTHOR OF WATER TO WINE**

"In *Apparent Faith*, Karl Forehand gently guides his readers through his journey of faith and reveals what many before him have begun to find: God is not a monster. God is wholly loving, truly good, and God, when it is all said and done, is just like Jesus. This is a book that will challenge many, but it is written with such care that readers will not be able to help but see the beauty within the pages. A thoroughly enjoyable and accessible read indeed."

**—MATTHEW J. DISTEFANO, AUTHOR OF 4 BOOKS AND CO-HOST OF THE HERETIC HAPPY HOUR PODCAST**

"In these pages Karl Forehand pulls back the veneer of superficiality and honestly reflects on his journey of struggle and faith. He courageously tells his story as a pastor who began to ask difficult questions within the narrow confines of the fundamentalist Christian faith he had always known. He discovers the beauty of God revealed in Jesus Christ, the personal God of trinitarian love, the God of endless creativity and moral goodness. His rediscovery of the ever-present God becomes a source of healing and transformation for Karl's heart and the centerpiece of his evolving beliefs about the nature of God, the Bible, the church, prayer, justice, war, parenting, and politics. Told in candor and reflection, Karl reflects on his life as a pastor and, more importantly, he reflects on his life as a parent, allowing his children to be his muse. This book will encourage and inspire you wherever you are on your faith journey."

**—DEREK VREELAND, DISCIPLESHIP PASTOR AT WORD OF LIFE CHURCH, ST. JOSEPH, MISSOURI AND AUTHOR OF BY THE WAY: GETTING SERIOUS ABOUT FOLLOWING JESUS**

"Reading *Apparent Faith* is like reading a journal: someone's touching and honest journal account of their journey towards a more Christlike God. Karl Forehand learned about the nature of God by taking a close look at the relationship between him and his children and shares those lessons with us. I'm thankful that Karl has shared his beautiful, painful, and honest journey with us. As he continued to walk in the darkness and shared his experiences with uncertainty and mystery, I couldn't help but think of Wendell Berry's words: *The mind that is not baffled is not employed / The impeded stream is the one that sings.* Thank you Karl for your gift!"

**—JOE BEACH, PASTOR AT AMAZING GRACE CHURCH**

"Karl's story is not theory. His curiosity and courage have led him and many others to dance in life in a better way. I have watched Karl walk through fear time and time again to find life. I hope this book inspires you to do the same."

—BRAD HILL, EXECUTIVE DIRECTOR OF HEARTCONNEXION SEMINARS, AUTHOR, AND PODCASTER

"Karl writes in a real, earthy, moving way that touches the heart of the reader. Thanks for sharing this."

—S. MARCIA ZISKA, OSB MOUNT ST. SCHOLASTICA, ATCHISON, KS.

"If I could somehow distill into words my story of being a father, husband, and a follower of Jesus, I am uncertain I would be able to do it better than Karl has here. This book gripped me, pulling emotions from me in the best ways. Karl, like so many of us, has leaned into Jesus and found something so beautiful and worth following—seeing beauty in both light and dark places."

—SETH PRICE, HOST OF CAN I SAY THIS AT CHURCH PODCAST

"For better or worse, many of us form our image of God from our relationship with our earthly father. In *Apparent Faith*, Karl Forehand makes a heartwarming and compelling case that God reveals just as much of Himself in and through our relationships with our own children—pointing us to a love without limits and hope without end. This book will help you discover the Father we all long for; subtly hidden within so many of the relationships of life."

—JASON ELAM, HOST OF THE MESSY SPIRITUALITY PODCAST

First Edition

Cover design and layout by Rafael Polendo (polendo.net)

ISBN 978-1-938480-44-7

This volume is printed on acid free paper and meets ANSI Z39.48 standards.

Printed in the United States of America

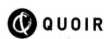 QUOIR

Published by Quoir
Orange, California

www.quoir.com

# APPARENT FAITH

## What Fatherhood Taught Me
## About the Father's Heart

### KARL FOREHAND

To my children
Jordan (J.D.), Abigail (Abbey), and Lily (L.B.)

and to my grandchildren
Hollyn and Jackson (J.B.)

# TABLE OF CONTENTS

# ACKNOWLEDGEMENTS

Life if interesting at times. This book heavily involves my children, who used to have a baby sitter named Tricia, who married a guy named Jeremiah Davis who grew up to be, among other things, an editor and formed Vanguard Publishing House. So, guess who did most of the editing on this book? The life of a writer is extremely interdependent on the necessary and vital work they do. At times I despise editors for changing my work, and at other times I want to kiss their feet. Kind of like most things in life, I guess. Here's to you Jeremiah! This book is better because of you!

As long as I have dreamed about being a writer, I have dreamed about having a publisher. To be honest, I didn't think it would ever happen. As I became acquainted with Keith Giles, he recommended talking to Rafael (Ralph) Polendo at Quoir Publishing. Surprise! He said yes! For a while, I kept sending cryptic messages to verify that it was indeed true! Quoir produces the popular podcast, Heretic Happy Hour, among other things. As I have come to know some of their writers like Matthew Distefano, Jamal Jivanjee, and the aforementioned Ketih Giles, I feel like I'm the luckiest writer in the world. They are exactly the right fit as they are challenging the same boundaries that I am challenging, and they are doing it well! I look forward to many years of doing this thing we're doing right now!

When I first met Brian Zahnd, I didn't know whether I would like him—let's just leave it at that. It still surprises me that I call Word of Life Church in St. Joseph, Missouri my home. I was never a charismatic before and I pastored smaller churches, but I have grown to love Brian and Peri Zahnd and Derek Vreeland and others of the pastors and members there. More than anything, I admire their courage. They are rejecting the certainty of pop Christianity and striking out on journeys to discover a more authentic faith. They are doing this individually and corporately to some extent. I respect them for having the courage to do this, while trying to preserve the church and care for the people involved. They don't complain about it, but I know it is not an easy journey. I am extremely thankful for my church and pastors even though I'm probably not the best member sometimes! *L'Chaim* my friends!

Dr. Paul Fitzgerald and his wife, Susanna, have served as guides to us at various times in our lives. Approximately 20 years ago, they led us through an immersive experience called Breakthrough where we felt like we gained a new lease on life. After a couple of decades of pastoral work, I needed to experience this process again and Laura and I enlisted them as guides once more. When I needed a friend and mentor, it was like Dr. Paul suddenly appeared in my life again. He never offers advice I don't ask for, but he is always there with just the right thing to say. I suspect it is because he is a few steps down the path on a similar journey as me. I appreciate Dr. Paul and Susanna and I consider them two of my closest friends. They are the type of people that genuinely spiritually reproduce and legitimately impact the world. They are the real deal in a world of imposters. I love you guys!

# FOREWORD

It has been a joy to journey with Karl and Laura as they explore the "wideness in God's mercy, like the wideness of the sea" even when it feels more like a wild ride into the unknown destination. Celtic Christians called this a "perigrinatio"—a passionate journey without a specific destination into the unknown that was as much an inner journey to discover their truest self in Christ.

The Forehand's family story reflects the risk we all face in suddenly waking up to see so clearly something to which we have been blind, and it can be quite troubling—light in darkness may be shocking and yet enticingly invite us to explore the unfamiliar. Being available to be surprised by God is key to deep spiritual growth beyond the limits of logic we feel gives us control.

John's Gospel begins by naming the resistance of darkness—our falsely-centered self and our collective cultural, political, economic false-self systems—and the blindness to which even the most intensely religious people are subject:

> "What came into existence was Life, and the Life was Light to live by. The Life-Light blazed out of the darkness; the darkness could not put it out...The Life-Light was the real thing: Every person entering Life he brings into Light. He was in the world, the world was there through him, and yet the world did not even notice. He came to his own people, but they did not want him."[1]

Sometimes deep intuitions resist our desire to stay safe and awaken us to more going on than our normal ego-centered awareness wants us to know. It can be shocking to see the beauty of something we have dismissed as unimaginable. We do not create those 'exceptional' moments, they are there stirring in us, calling us to embrace doubt as a doorway to deeper faith.

The courageous act to follow our intuitive knowing—rather than analyze the experience as an observer—may shake our ordinary life-planning to the core. It is likely that we will be tempted to dismiss them as irrational, a 'bad dream,' stilly, or crazy. Our current path's predictable safety can make the journey feel that too much is at risk to allow the intrusion of those Divine moments to register as more real than our illusions.

The paradox is that embracing and acting on those 'break through' moments can bring renewed strength, courage, meaning and energy for life. And, as Karl's story illustrates, it also brings a time of 'deconstruction,' a feeling that the very foundations of what we have assumed to be true are being undermined. Talking to friends and family can feel too risky and often result in their attempting to rescue us from ourselves. Too quickly this can turn into rejection if our changes threaten their working illusions.

Sometimes our courage fails us, and we turn back to the comfortable path we think we know. Yet, it may not be possible to completely deaden the yearning that revisits us in strange ways. Once we begin, the temptation to go back is very real. There is strength in finding some welcoming souls who are a few steps ahead and experiencing more trust in the Mystery than our logic and rational skills to return to control.

May Karl, Laura and the Forehand family's journey inspire you to journey into the wideness and wildness of grace.

John O'Donohue describes the challenge we are all invited to explore:

> "If we can somehow bring the difficult things with us into the realm and light of our souls, it is unbelievable the healing that will achieve itself in us. I think that we are infinitely greater than our minds and we are infinitely more than our images of ourselves. One of the sad things today is that so many people are frightened by the wonder of their own presence. They are dying to tie themselves into a system, a role, or to an image, or to a predetermined identity that other people have settled on for them. This identity may be totally at variance with the wild energies that are rising inside their souls. Many of us get very afraid and we eventually compromise. We settle for something that is safe, rather than engaging the danger and the wildness that is in our own hearts. We should never forget that death is waiting for us."[2]

Godspeed,

—**Paul Fitzgerald, D.Min.**
www.heartconnexion.org
drpaul@heartconnexion.org

# INTRODUCTION

It started with a simple statement: "Maybe I am wrong."

Now, this wasn't something I said because I had just quit my job, or gone on a 3-month sabbatical, or suffered through a midlife crisis. Nothing that dramatic. But I was beginning to have my suspicions and doubts; and eventually found myself losing confidence in the faith that I had invested my life in.

I was a bi-vocational pastor spending most of my free time pursuing "The Lord's Work." But what I most wanted out of life at this time was to be a little more sure of what I seemed so sure about.

Faith is, after all, a kind of assurance. There's a measure of comfort in knowing the Truth. As I had learned as a pastor, Evangelicalism requires a fair amount of certainty about what you believe. But it can also provoke questions in other areas of your life. These you can either ignore or address. Most tend to ignore them, I think. But I started to address them.

Over the course of several years, I began to question everything. Were my beliefs right? How did I determine this? What if it is not right? What if it is? Maybe I am wrong?

As I asked myself these questions, my faith began to crack at the foundations like a towering skyscraper and it began to sway. Repeatedly, I found myself in the role of an apologist. Eventually asking myself, "Why do I always have to defend those particular beliefs?" And again, "What if I am wrong?"

Maybe in a rush to be so certain about my faith, as an evangelical, I determined some things incorrectly. I started to wonder if some things don't really require such certainty. Maybe the answers would come later? Still, I felt compelled to probe a little deeper.

Around this time, I had some health issues and implemented some corrective actions involving diet and exercise. Going through that, I was so excited to be feeling better that I wanted to tell others what I was experiencing. I've always felt that our lives involve body, soul and spirit and we often neglect what we don't understand.

To my surprise, I received a lot of criticism, even ridicule, from people in my former denomination. They would say things like "you talk about nutrition too much" and would laugh whenever I talked about making changes to my diet or exercise habits. Maybe I didn't *need* to convince them, but it did hurt a little to be minimized. Eventually, I realized my change made some people uncomfortable, so I stopped talking about the changes my wife and I had made in our lifestyle. This was not really a spiritual thing, but it was part of our gradual process of disconnecting from the system we were in.

After becoming the clichéd, irritating health food nut, I committed the next big sin: I discovered yoga, and I loved it! In my limited experience, I am convinced of its health benefits, and have continued to enjoy it intermittently for several years. What really surprised me was when one of the leaders in the church refused to take communion from me until he could address this "yoga issue" with me. Later that week, he invited me to dinner.

The conversation did not resolve his frustration, and it only served to raise my level of disappointment with the state of the church. I don't fault this person, but it left me wondering, "Why are people not happy for me when my health is improving?" Again, I asked the question, "Maybe I am wrong," or "Maybe I was wrong all along."

These were just surface issues. On a deeper level, I felt like I was pretending to be happy and being pressured to ascribe to things I was losing faith in, and at the same time I was beginning to feel estranged from the communities we once drew strength from.

Eventually, it became clear to me that I needed to get outside my role as a pastor and discover what I truly believed so that I could find peace and be able to express that peace to others. I longed to go deeper into the faith I confessed. The statement, "Maybe I am wrong" had changed from a question into a conviction. I was no longer the apologist or fraud I feared I might be. I was me.

Several months later, I resigned from the church I was a part of. This was more like a divorce than a simple resignation from office. Most of the people we knew in those circles stop communicating with us completely. That's when I began to examine everything. I knew I needed people I cared about in my life to walk with me on this journey. I reconnected with an old friend, Dr. Paul Fitzgerald, who runs an immersive program called Breakthrough. My wife Laura and I had been through the program before and trusted him. His teaching on shame and grace had been instrumental in my life already. That first time through his program we probably were more focused on marital issues—this time we needed help with the second half of our life.

Dr. Paul reads a copious number of books. When we invited him on our journey, he recommended books to get us started. Some of the more memorable were:

- *Sinners in the Hands of a Loving God,* Brian Zahnd
- *The Bible Tells Me So,* Peter Enns
- *A More Christlike God, Brad Jersak*
- *Falling Upward,* Richard Rohr

I remember one morning having breakfast with Dr. Paul and his wife as they told us about Wm. Paul Young and the film based on his book, *The Shack.* The intensity in their voice encouraged us to see this movie. We almost felt like we might be the only persons in the world that had not seen it by the tone of their voices. We watched the movie later that week and bought tickets to see the author speak in person. That movie, and Paul Young's stories, left us speechless.

Something truly was awakened in us that had been dormant for a long time. It had been awhile since I read and considered such challenging ideas—I was hungry for more!

As I started to read those books that Dr. Paul had recommended to us, I found that, while all of these authors were further down the road than I was, they all seemed to be on the same journey towards a common destination. A journey towards a God who was less violent and retributive than I had been taught and a faith that was more about love and mercy. My long-held assumptions and traditions were being challenged and I felt like I was ready to let go but I did not know how.

Eventually I met Brian and Peri Zahnd and began attending the church they pastored—Word of Life Church, in St. Joseph, MO. This was an important part of the journey.

Later, I read Paul Young's book, *Lies We Believe About God*. It was what I was looking for, but not entirely ready to hear. Some of what I read I believed but some of it I immediately dismissed. As I would read the book, I would often catch myself saying, "Wow!", then pause and ponder what I had just read before moving on. I would do this repeatedly—opening, closing, opening, closing—rinse and repeat, until I got to the end of the book.

Many of my long-held beliefs were challenged, but a grander shift was happening in me. After reading the book and thinking through all the things I was considering, I made the following assessment:

> "Some of my beliefs lead to a natural conclusion that I am better than God. As a parent I do things a certain way (and I am not perfect). My belief system says that God does things or did things a certain way. My belief is in question because it leads to a conclusion that God is worse than me."

That's when it all began to change for me. Maybe I am wrong about hell, particularly the idea that God punishes people forever for rejecting him. Still, I can't help but wonder how God can love the world, be so unendingly full of grace and mercy, and have so much vengeful anger that his anger results in people suffering for eternity? That feels like a contradiction of his character that I can't simply ignore any longer.

I began to wonder how a perfect God could be a worse Father than me. I kept coming back to the Sophia scene from *The Shack* and asking myself, "Which of my children I would eternally torment for not believing in or disobeying me or just continuing to be rebellious?" I determined I could not—I cannot—I will not!

My presuppositions shattered and I determined something was going to have to change. If you are anything like I used to be, I see you that you are poised to run. I understand how you feel as these kinds of considerations used to frighten me as well. I felt the same way, but I stayed on the journey long enough to satisfy my curiosity and find some peace. I don't ask that you accept everything I say—just journey with me.

One final note. You may notice a lack of Scriptural reference in this book. You can find answers for that in the chapter titled "The Bible," but I do not recommend jumping ahead just yet. The main reason I chose not to have a lot of references to the Bible is I feel Scripture has become a weapon to defend our inherited and predetermined agenda instead of a fertile soil for our faith. Scripture is an important part of my life and undergirds much of my journey, but what follows is not a theological debate and not in any way intended to defend a certain set of beliefs. This is my journey and I offer these stories that are sacred to me that you may somehow share the journey with me.

The path ahead of you may or may not be shrouded in mystery, however there are many bumps and surprising turns hidden in the veil called faith. It is easier to remain complacent and not move forward. Stability and tradition can seem to be less of a challenge than what is ahead—less threatening if you are not running pell-mell into the chaos.

Faith, we are told, is the assurance of things hoped for, the conviction of things unseen. But what happens when the path takes you on a journey into the darker side of faith, each step challenging prior convictions even as it is building new ones?

Nevertheless, we must press forward. Let us walk together, you and I, and in so doing find peace.

—Karl J. Forehand, 2019

## Section 1

# *DISCOVERIES*

# GOD'S DISPOSITION TOWARDS US

The biggest surprise of parenthood came during a late-night meetup at an IHOP restaurant with my family. My wife, Laura, and I had orchestrated a get together with our children (not an easy task with three adult children). Sometime early in the conversation with them I realized, "They are teaching me. This is going to make me a better man." They were not lecturing me and they probably didn't even have an agenda, but I was learning from the conversation my wife and I were having with them.

As a young adult I had dreamed about all the things I would teach my children. I remember preparing to answer their questions so they would look at me with wonder and amazement. I imagined them marveling at my theology degree infused brilliance, replying at my every turn with, "Dad, you are a masterful thinker and wise sage. Please, share more!" I was a little disappointed at how little they asked me for advice; mostly, they just watched what I did.

Even more surprising than their lack of need for my wisdom was their apparent ability to learn for themselves. I taught them to think for themselves early on, and I was humbled when they learned on their own. A steady march from there led to independence and I heard myself thinking, "It will not be long before they do not need me at all." Of course, that is the goal, but the perceived rejection still hurt a little.

Somewhere in my Fatherhood journey, I was inspired to compare my relationship with God to my role as a father. Is not God's relationship with me supposed to be a lot like a father and a child? God can be imagined as many things, but when I compared him to my experience as a father, I knew he was showing me a deeper part of himself, a true part of himself. I knew God would not turn his back on us because I would never turn my back on my children.

A common belief among many Christians is that God turns away from us when we sin. It was imagined that even Jesus experienced this on the cross when he absorbed our sins. The assumption is that the Father is so holy he cannot look at sin—so he separates or hides Himself from us.

*I told each of them several times throughout their childhood and beyond, "No matter what you do, I will never change how I feel about you." When they made bad choices, it did not drive me away from them—it made me want to draw closer.*

As a father, I find this hard to accept. One of the primary reasons is, as a created being, I promised my children I would never leave them.

I told each of them several times throughout their childhood and beyond, "No matter what you do, I will never change how I feel about you." When they made bad choices, it did not drive me away from them—it made me want to draw closer. I know people that have disowned their children because they made mistakes. This seems selfish to me because it is usually the parent trying to avoid embarrassment. Although I understand what it is like when my children made mistakes, it doesn't seem like love to turn away from them in their distress.

In the creation story, after Adam and Eve made a bad choice for themselves, they hid like all children are prone to do when they realize their mistake. Out of love as a Father, God came looking for Adam—God did not pull away nor allow them to remain hidden. He went looking for them. Prodigal sons and daughters worry in shame over past mistakes, while the Father's heart in us propels us to search for them, to run to them with arms open wide.

Another area that can be confusing to Christians is "God's work." My children were not always perfect like they are now (both of us are laughing right now). Whenever I would ask them to take out the trash, they would do the "wobbly legs" dance. With the dance, they were trying to communicate that they were so tired they could not possibly do one more thing or they would collapse under the weight of their many burdens. It goes without saying that they had been sitting in the same position for more than an hour, but rationalizing things like that will sometimes drive you crazy as a parent. Often, I just took out the trash myself to avoid the battle.

When I was a young parent, I imagined that all my children would lighten my load, that they would learn to work and do their chores. All my children are good workers, but they never did much work for me. After all, most kids just want to relax when they came home—just like I did. They did their work at school, and when they got older had their own jobs. My children did not want to be my slaves--they wanted to be part of the family. I believe we need to examine our views of how God views our service. Is it an expected duty where we are "used" by God or is it what we do out of love for others? I think my children are just now understanding how this works in a family.

If you have ever been to a church service, then you know that most church literature is packed with missional injunctions about being "used" by God. Sadly, it is a common theme especially among evangelicals. "Here am I, send me" and being "used by God" are common themes we hear hammered out of the pulpit, all whilst faintly on the organ "Onward Christian Soldiers" is being played—our cue to march forward and do God's work. Try to suggest this to an abuse victim, apply being "used by God" to your children—say out loud "I want to use my children for my purposes." The Father's heart roars like a lion in protest because no one likes to be used. It is too easy for use to become abuse. I do not think this is the way God sees his Family, nor how Christ sees his Bride, the Church. God did not create us to use us. I can no longer accept this.

I like the way Bob Goff approaches this issue in his book *Love Does*:

> "I think a father's job, when it is done best, is to get down on both knees, lean over his children's lives, and whisper, 'Where do you want to go?' Every day God invites us on the same kind of adventure. It is not a trip where He sends us a rigid itinerary, He simply invites us. God asks what it is He's made us to love, what it is that captures our attention, what feeds that deep indescribable need of our souls to experience the richness of the world He made. And then, leaning over us, He whispers, 'Let's go do *that* together.'"

Discipline is another area that can confuse us about God. Two of my children were easy to scare into submission when they were out of control with only a strong look. The other child was very stubborn and once destroyed her room because she was mad. I can still remember the stare of my oldest daughter. For whatever reason, I was determined to get her to eat her supper. I am sure she was not starving to death and there likely was not a good reason except that she was defying me. I am sure it was not the first time and probably not the last. Out of frustration, I spanked her. She did not cry—she did not run to her room—all she did was stare at me! I remember walking away. Like many things in Fatherhood, the moment you think you've figured it out, the family throws you a curve.

I realized that discipline has it limits and what my children often needed more than to be disciplined was my understanding and compassion. They were often frustrated more than rebellious, more confused than confrontational, and in need of grace, mercy, and compassion more than punishment. They needed me to be more restorative than retributive. They needed me to lead them home.

**They were often frustrated more than rebellious, more confused than confrontational, and in need of grace, mercy, and compassion more than discipline.**

Sometimes they really needed me to listen and it was in those moments that I learned God's discipline may be something different than what I imagined. It is more obvious to me now that God is not a god that is waiting to punish me.

I know I taught my children many things, but sitting in that IHOP restaurant with my wife and children, I saw that most of what they learned from me they learned more by my example—not my verbal instruction. And I can delight in my children because of that. And maybe that is what family is all about, finding delight in our children as we spend time with them until they enter adulthood and do the same. I know one thing for sure, I cannot imagine a life without my wife and children in it and I am learning that God feels the same way towards his family too.

---

## FOR FURTHER THOUGHT

Reflect on the statements below. Don't overthink it, just let it flow. You can analyze it later.

1. Describe your previous perception of how God feels about you and contrast that with how your perception of that is changing?

   • Is God looking down at you or across?

   • How big is God is relation to you?

   • Is God distant or near?

   • What colors do you see?

   • What is the primary feeling you are having about this?

   • What else do you see in the picture?

2. What are several words that summarize your thoughts about this chapter or what is a quote you would like to remember?

# ORIGINAL GOOD
# AND PARENTS

Our second grandchild was born recently. He was born via C-section eight weeks early. Emotions flowed over me like a river when I considered meeting my new grandson. I was overwhelmed with joy for my granddaughter who was born a year earlier, and I now wondered, "Would I have the same feelings for Jackson?" When it finally did happen, when I finally looked at his face, I thought, "Perfection!" What I mean is not that he was perfect, but that he was innocent and good and precious. And he was exactly who he was supposed to be. I did not see evil in his demeanor. In a special way that every parent knows, I saw God in his eyes. Once again, I was blown away.

In the creation story, God looked at creation and said several times, "That is good." After he created man, he looked at his creation and said, "That is very good." When I look at a baby, I think, "This is good!" Babies are a miracle—such an expression of innocence—a thing of beauty. They are, inside and out, "very good."

My granddaughter, Hollyn, appears to be very determined like her mother. Like Abbey, she sometimes refuses to do certain things like wear her gloves. I think my daughter already knows so I do not tell her, "Give up, you're not going to win the battle—it is not that important." But there are many other times when she is not being stubborn. And, that is when I see the goodness! When Hollyn sits and listens to an Avett Brothers song with me, my mind goes back to a picture of Abbey with her grandpa. They were very close. And in both of their eyes I see pure delight, I see mystery, I see all the good things I love about God.

As a pastor, I had the privilege to hold dozens of babies. Many times, I was the first person to hold the baby after the mother had given the first feeding. My eyes were always drawn to the tiny little toes and fingernails that seemed so perfect. Occasionally though, I was lucky enough to get a quick glance as the young soul blinked open their eyes. I am told that what they see at this point is blurry, unfocused and limited.

## But what I saw was clear! This creation of God was nothing but goodness, purity and sweetness.

But what I saw was clear! This creation of God was nothing but goodness, purity and sweetness. You do not have to prompt people to "ooh" and "ahh" over a baby; they do it spontaneously because what they are seeing is good!

In many religions, there is a core belief that we are originally bad. I do not think we can deduce that from the creation story though, and I cannot conclude it from looking at my own children. God the Father does not hide behind Jesus to look at us any more than I hide behind my children to see my grandchildren. I believe he looks at us like I looked at my grandson, Jackson. He looks at us like I see my granddaughter, Hollyn, when I sing Avett Brothers' songs to her.

My children have introduced me to podcasts. To me, they are like the new cassette tapes, except I do not have to lug them around with me to then get destroyed when I leave them in the floorboard of the car. Recently, I was listening to Richard Rohr on a podcast and the only thing I can remember (and I am paraphrasing here) is this:

"God is not trying to create a new version of ourselves because we were originally bad. God is trying to remove the false self we have accumulated and return us to our true self that is originally good."

I have been conditioned by the things that have happened to me. When children made fun of me or adults harshly scolded me, it seemed to build up a layer of shame that caused me to change my view of myself and the world. When I made mistakes, as we all do, the world did not always respond in healthy, restorative ways. Our world is very retributive and when I exchanged insult for insult with the world, it only caused me to build up a false self that was nothing like the infant I saw in the hospital. I realized that I did not know the true self inside me. I forgot that I was once a newborn that my mother carried down the stairs of a clinic in Edmond, OK. I failed to remember that I once had perfect little toes that deserved a second glance. I forgot that she once looked into my eyes and said, "This is good!"

I once wrote a story called, "I Wanted Him to Score a Touchdown." It was about when I watched my son play football. My assessment of his interest in football was that he enjoyed being on the team more than playing the game. He was a jokester and loved to make people happy. In retrospect, those are much better life qualities than succeeding at a game, but in this part of the world it is easy to get wrapped in all of it.

But there he was on the two-yard line. He was a blocking back and did not carry the ball—instead he was always all-to-happy to clear the way for his friend. For some reason, I knew he was going to get the ball that day and I was ecstatic. "I just want him to score one touchdown," I thought, as I screamed at the top of my lungs, "Go, go, go!" Sure enough, he took the hand-off but very soon felt the wrath of the opposing defensive line. My heart sank. I felt so bad for him as he fell inches short. "Can I get a measurement?" Moments later, I observed another impassioned parent. This guy's son was one of the biggest guys on the team which was one of the reasons for the team's success. As I watched him live and die with his son on the field, I began to wonder whether we were doing the right thing. His commentary was sometimes encouraging, but other times it was downright shaming and a little too harsh for the situation. I wonder whether we were encouraging these young men or frustrating them?

What would God do if he watched a football game with all his children?

When I was a young parent, I thought it was my job to push my children to be "more." Whatever that means! I felt like they needed me to focus on their performance and try to push them to new heights. Even now with my children all adults, it is tempting to go too far with this model. When I think about how things will look and how it will reflect on me, I can very easily push them, not to excellence, but to frustration.

I was taught that God has a very high standard. This "mark" or expectation is basically unreachable. But it goes further than that. God knows that this standard is unreachable, but it drives him insane when we cannot meet this standard. It makes him so angry that he dreams of tormenting us forever. It reminds me of parents in the stands of athletic events dreaming of their children's performance and losing their minds when they fail to perform! "This is not what we expect from you," they would yell at the top of their lungs. I used to believe that was how God felt about our sin. Then, I noticed what Jesus did. I saw that he looked upon people with compassion. I saw that he said, "Father, forgive them, for they do not know what they are doing." Every parent of teenagers should learn that phrase.

We do not go to as many sporting events these days. Someday, I am sure we will be asked to attend some type of performance for the grandchildren. My greatest hope is that I will be a better observer than I have been in the past. I hope I will scold less and encourage more. I hope I will not generate unrealistic expectations of my grandchildren, but instead learn to delight in them like God delights in me. I hope I can learn to expect them to be who they truly are.

Life is full of firsts. With children, there is the first word, the first step, the first tooth, the first date, the first day of school. But there is also the first time they rebel or stay out past curfew or tell you "you are the worst parent ever!" I was trying to remember specific instances of their rebellion. The truth is, for me, it is very hard to remember those instances of their defiance or poor performance. At the time, they seemed devastating, and although I remember the emotions of embarrassment and shame, I cannot remember the actual stories. What I do remember are the times of reconciliation afterward.

My best memories of interacting with my children all end with me admitting I was wrong. I remember once when my daughter, Lily, confronted me. Lily has always been very intelligent and has grown to be a strong, intelligent woman, and mother of my grandson. I know it is not accurate, but I remember her speaking without a breath for 20 minutes. I remember feeling like what she said was very disrespectful, but then something made me listen a little closer. What I eventually discerned from her speech is that both of us have expectations in our relationship. One side of me wanted to just say, "Listen, you need to be more respectful," but, the other side of me realized there was something very important to what she was saying. When I finally stopped living in my expectation, I heard her and I was able to eke out, "I am sorry!" Years later, we would have a very similar conversation. This time the conversation was even more critical and even more direct, but it ended elegantly. All my children at one time or another have told me that one of the best things they remember from their childhood was when "dad" would admit he was wrong.

As my children grew older, I learned some of my expectations were unrealistic. But, even when my expectations were realistic and achievable, my children sometimes missed the mark. When I adopted a more Christlike attitude, I found I had more compassion for them (not more anger toward them). If I can grow into that, I am sure God is already like that.

> **When I adopted a more Christlike attitude, I found that I had more compassion for them (not more anger toward them). If I can grow into that, I am sure God is already like that.**

Parenting scared me to death. Early on, when I was searching for tips on being a good father, I found this verse, "Fathers, do not provoke your children to anger." I read books, listened to speakers, and digested all sorts of advice from people. But nothing seemed as appropriate as this one single verse. I knew this because I had been provoked by adults in my own life. I knew how it affected me and I did not want to make the same mistakes with my children. It was a certainty that they would be angry at me at times, but there was no need for me to provoke them unnecessarily.

Since I had no idea how to be a good father, I defaulted to this rule often. I tried to ask myself, "Is this going to frustrate my children?" If it is going to frustrate them, then is it worth doing? Laura would often remind me of this rule, and I applied it when Lily and I "discussed" things and I am sure I will apply it to my relationship with my grandchildren. Children will be frustrated enough when they challenge authority and go through the process of maturing and growing in their understanding. Obviously, wisdom is involved, but sometimes it is wise to say nothing.

**The lingering question in my mind is, "Why would God set up a system that is doomed from the start?" Why would he give us an unreachable goal and then be out-of-his-mind angry about the fact that we cannot reach it?**

The lingering question in my mind is, "Why would God set up a system that is doomed from the start?" Why would he give us an unreachable goal and then be out-of-his-mind angry about the fact when we cannot reach it? That would be more like me at my worst than like God who is supposed to be the best. I have seen little league parents scar their children with words. God is not like parents with unrealistic expectations. I remembered Jesus at his baptism and transfiguration when the Father said, "This is my beloved son in whom I am well pleased." I do not think this is because of Jesus' performance—I think it is because of the decision the Father makes to delight in and love the Son. It is the natural disposition of the trinity. God is love—God is patient—God is kind.

God is better than me.

## FOR FURTHER THOUGHT

Reflect on the statements below. Don't overthink it, just let it flow. You can analyze it later.

1. Describe some images you once had about yourself that you now know are false.

2. What does your true self look like?

3. Which version of you are you most like?

4. Imagine seeing yourself as a baby or at a younger age.

   • What would you say to that version of you?

   • What would you do? Pick him/her up? Give them a kiss? Recite something?

5. What are several words that summarize your thoughts about this chapter or what is a quote you would like to remember?

# GOD IS GOOD?

I saw a t-shirt today that included the words, "God is good." If you have ever been to an evangelical church, you have heard the phrase there as well:

*Pastor: "God is good!"*
*Congregation "All the time!"*
*Pastor: "And all the time..."*
*Congregation: "God is good!"*

Even at a reserved church, you might hear some applause as the congregation looks around as if to say, "And we are pretty good too!" Warm thoughts of denominationalism, even patriotism, spread throughout the room as everyone thinks "It is good to be us...God is good, and God is for us!" In the past few months, I have heard the phrase a lot from church goers, typically after a hospital visit, surviving an illness, or making money. To put it simply, this was typically used at a time when things went the way the person wanted them to.

Now, when I hear the phrase, I am more apt to ask, "why" and "what motivates you to think that way?" I know I am not alone in thinking this. Did God reward me for something I did, or did I pray in exactly the right way? Can I get what I want from God? What if the person did not make it through the surgery? What if the diagnosis was cancer and not a miracle? Do we question God and ourselves when things do not go the way we want?

When our children were infants, they depended on us for everything. Recently, I watched my daughter take care of her son. It was exhausting to watch. Laura is very good about taking the load off my daughter—holding the baby and helping her when she is around—but I am still too mesmerized by the whole process to respond quick enough to help.

I notice some chemistry between our daughter and grandson, but mostly his affection is limited to his basic needs. Laura and I (mostly Laura) could make the hunger pains of our children go away or clean up the discomfort of a messy diaper or just put them in a warm, comfortable place to sleep. They could not verbalize it yet, but because we met their basic needs, mom and dad were "good!"

When our children were toddlers and small children, I was good because I could amuse them for brief periods of time with toys and funny faces. I was their ticket to the magical places like the park and the ice cream shop. Although they were learning to feed themselves, they still relied on me and trusted me to bring them food that tasted good and made them healthy. Laura and I were the trusted providers of sickness relief, and the official dispensers of "ouchie" comfort. Life was evolving, but the theme continued.

Even as teenagers, I received a similar response. In some ways, it got more pronounced because then they knew what they were doing. Chauffeuring teenage girls to various events was one of the most frightening things I have ever done. I was consistently afraid of saying the wrong thing (which was very easy to do) or being too silly. Nearly anything with teenage girls can "ruin their life." Once when I asked, "How did I do?", after taking her friends out for her birthday, she responded, "You did okay!"

What I heard from my daughter was "You are good." What I could faintly hear from heaven was, "This is my beloved son." This is just one of things that, as a parent, made me feel good and pathetic at the same time.

Their lives became less dependent on me, and occasionally they would humble themselves enough to come out of their bedroom to acknowledge me. Unfortunately, that was only when they needed to ask for money! If you are a young parent, let me assure you about the teenage years. There will be a few times your teenagers will admit you are "good!" The bad news is it will only be when they want money or the keys to the car. You will in fact be "the greatest," but only for an instant. I have at times been acknowledged on Facebook by my teenage children, but I'm not sure it was worth it for what I had to go through to get the scraps of their thankfulness. It was more like manipulation.

There was a period where my children became adults and did not need me. I always dreamed that when they moved out on their own one day, they would write me letters to thank me for all the lessons I had taught them and the thousands of dollars I had "invested" in their education. I go get the mail every day now, the short walk to our mailbox is exhilarating. I feel a short spike of anticipation when the mail carrier comes. *Maybe this will be the day I find the letter I have been looking for.* The letter never comes, and I am left standing at the mailbox holding offers for life insurance and bills. My children are not the spontaneous note-writing type.

As they got a little older and more mature, my children did acknowledge in their own individual ways, that they thought we were "good" in their eyes. Since they are at least partially like me, it was not a big emotional event. Most of the time they say it in the little things, moments of weakness when they slip up and let it be known that we were at least okay (good) in their eyes. It was not when we gave them something or let them do something or helped them get something they wanted--it was just because they took some reflection and recognized what was "good" about us was the relationship that somehow survived the middle school years (affectionately known as hell to any parent with a daughter).

And there it is, what's good about God is what's good about family—it is the relationship. In my mind, God is not just good when things go well, God is better when things are going the worst.

### God is not just good when things go well, God is better when things are going the worst.

As a pastor, I listened to people pray for miracles and thank God for healings. Often, I would turn to see the medical professional that probably dedicated their life and might have worked hard all night to help this person silently slip out of the room. I wondered if they resented God for getting all the credit while they probably got all the blame when it went badly. Often, I want to say thanks to the medical community as I thank God for his relationship with me as I went through the thing that caused me to say, "God is good."

I think if we only point up to the sky when we score a touchdown, we are going to remain spiritual teenagers. If we shout "God is good" only when our bellies are full, our diapers are clean, and the Spiderman nightlight in our bedrooms keeps away the bad guys, we should probably admit we are still infants, still taking a bottle every now and then, and most of what we accomplish is because daddy does it for us. Instead of looking around the church to congratulate ourselves we should realize we are all still wearing diapers and being fed spiritual milk. We still think God is good, but only when he loans us the car.

This past weekend, I had an unusually rich experience at something called Souljourners, which is training for being a spiritual director. In addition to learning how to listen to people (directing), we also experienced direction from the Benedictine Sisters who supervise the program. Sister Marcia is my spiritual director. She is wise, and patient and kind and occasionally offers some advice. On one occasion, she recommended a place she knew of nearby called the "International Forest of Friendship."

This park has trees from every state in the union and several foreign countries. I walked along snapping pictures of trees from states I know people would be interested in. It was so relaxing and refreshing! I stopped several times just to reflect and meditate on the quiet beauty. The "good"ness of God was most evident there. Then, something happened. As I was snapping a few pictures and thinking about leaving, I dropped my phone and broke the screen. If you know me, you know how attached I am to my phone and how devastating this could possibly be. As I paced around, wondering how I could get my phone fixed, I noticed an opening in the forest. It was kind of a walkway leading down to a circular cul-de-sac in the trees. The horseshoe bench that stood at the end of walkway beckoned to me to sit under the canopy of fall leaves that occasionally dropped to kiss the earth.

I sat in the middle of the bench and pulled out my broken phone. I was able to navigate to YouTube and turn on a song

I had recently discovered. It was a song of prayer called "The Cherokee Morning Song." I have grown to love the song, but it resonated so much more in the shadow of those trees. I felt rooted and grounded to the earth and I muttered to myself, "I am a part of this", and I thought, "This is a part of me." As my broken phone chanted "We n' de ya ho" (I am of the Great Spirit), my soul felt a kinship to God's creation. I thought, "This is truly good, and I am simply happy to be here."

Later, when I listened to a spiritual director meticulously apply her 30 plus years of experience to people seeking wisdom and discernment, I thought "God is good." When I saw people care for each other, it reminded me that God *is* good—but not because he made my path easier or gave me something which made me feel better. God is good--in relationship. An embrace more than a handout.

God is good when two people pray together in relationship—not just when it turns out the way they prayed. God is good when two people hold each other in turmoil-not just when the turmoil goes away. God is good because of and through relationship.

I have often wondered what my children say to their friends. Maybe they tell others, "Our parents are good", and their friends say, "All the time..." I would guess probably not. Today, I do not need to go out and check the mail for a letter I know will not be there anymore. The bills and offers still come often enough. I do not need a letter now because I can feel in their hugs, "This is good!"

All the time, my children, all the time!

## FOR FURTHER THOUGHT

Reflect on the statements below. Don't overthink it, just let it flow. You can analyze it later.

1. What does it say about us if we think God is only good when we get what we want?

2. What does it say about God if he randomly blesses or curses?

3. What are several words that summarize your thoughts about this chapter or what is a quote you would like to remember?

# WHAT GOD IS LIKE

About the time my children entered high school, they began to have questions. Occasionally, they or one of their friends would pose a challenging question that was hard for me to answer. These inquiries and concerns were part of what motivated me to ask those same questions of myself. I am eternally grateful because, in a way, they helped launch me on this journey to find a more genuine view of God. The way I interacted with them changed my views about God, some of the things that I assumed about God did not align with my own parenting. I am not God, but, I thought, God must be better than me.

To this day, I am the first one up on Christmas morning. Laura had a certain methodical way of doing things and it made her crazy when I would wake up the children early. This would always throw a monkey wrench into Christmas mornings at the Forehand's because I wanted everyone to hurry up and open their gifts. My family of origin was somewhat poor, and we did not always get a lot of gifts at Christmas. The idea of another being out there dropping off gifts out of the goodness of his heart and rewarding me for being "good" was enticing. Like many people, I love Christmas and Santa Claus was an early reference point for many of my views of God.

Santa Claus pairs up with many of the traditional views of God. After all, Santa Claus is always watching us to see if we have been good or bad. He keeps a list of all those things, checks it twice to see if we have been naughty or nice. I remember my mom reminding me, "Santa Claus is coming soon." My mind made the connection, "So I better be good for goodness sake!"

I also grew up in a male dominated, authoritarian type of religion. The leaders usually believed in capital, corporal punishment. They had little sympathy for those who committed crimes or disobeyed the rules at home. I do not remember ever being abused, but I most likely attached this angry, retributive image I witnessed to God. I heard vengeful sermons like the retelling of Jonathan Edwards, *Sinners in the Hands of an Angry God*, and made the connection that God is angry, vengeful, and must be appeased. This misperception can be understandable since much of the Old Testament was written in a period of human history where gods needed to be satisfied. The only logical face to put on God was the face of wrath—he could never quite be happy until he enacted some sort of violence. In this model, it is easy to put the face of Zeus onto God where God appears to be an imposing figure ready to hurl lightning bolts toward the earth at any time. Many of the stories of the Old Testament, if taken literally, seem to reinforce this image of God as Zeus-like and his temperament to be one of anger, retribution, and wrath.

In Bible college, I began to read the Bible for myself. When I studied the New Testament more intently, I discovered something interesting. I found evidence of a God that exhibited qualities of mercy, love, and forgiveness. This realization left me with questions and confusion. How could God be for loving my neighbor and still condone acts of genocide and slavery? Even penal substitutionary atonement still hints that God must perform some act of violence to appease his anger and it left me wondering why the whole system was so retributory. Could God not just forgive us without having to hurt something or someone? I know that most evangelicals would say that God is so holy that he has to have a sacrifice to pay for it. But didn't several people, including Jesus, say that sacrifice was not really what God desired? At that time, I subdued my questions and found a way to excuse some of the things I did not understand for the sake of certainty. But I couldn't escape the question and I continued to wonder.

## Could not God just forgive us without having to hurt something or someone?

After a certain age, my children stopped believing in Santa Claus. When I spoke of the mythical being, they would lean over to me and whisper, "You know Santa Claus is not real." Even though I stopped believing in Santa Claus, part of me wanted to retain this view of God as the eternal gift giver and the methodology that if I was good enough, I would receive good things, because I was acceptable.

This model began to break down when I had children. I noticed that often I would find myself in a situation where I had to withhold gifts from them even when they were good, and I needed to give them good things even when they did not deserve it. In short, there were more important principles than getting something periodically and being "nice" in order to win the favor of Jolly old Saint Nick.

I remember distinctly losing my temper a few times. I am mostly even-tempered, but occasionally I would lose it. I can still remember the look on the faces of Laura and our children when this would happen. I would always think the same thing, "This is not accomplishing anything noble." Laura and the children might have responded to my immediate demands, but I still did some damage that was going to take time to repair. This did not motivate them to be better people or teach them any substantial lesson, it just caused them to be afraid of me and to trust me a little less.

Every time this happened, it chipped away at my view of God as vengeful and angry. This was the worst disposition for me as a parent and it never produced positive results. I began to realize that getting my children to do what I wanted was not substantial unless their hearts and minds were changed. Fear, retribution, and anger are usually rooted in immaturity. They are incredibly effective, but for the wrong reasons, and they often leave residual damage. I began to lose faith in a God who looked like this. I began to see and understand that God was more like what I was learning in the New Testament.

### Fear, retribution, and anger are usually rooted in immaturity.

I do not remember who instigated the discussions. Most often it was Laura saying, "Why not sit down and talk to him?" She was referring to my only son, Jordan. So, the discussion began something like this, "You have done this thing that upset us, and we really should lock you up in a dungeon, take away your stuff, and never let you out until it is time for you to graduate and leave for somewhere else, but I am going to give you another chance." I would say this is grace and mercy and love because I loved him enough to give him something he did not deserve by not giving him what he did deserve. Do not get me wrong, this was not an everyday thing. I am far from perfect, but this seemed to be much closer to Christ-like and a better image of God than one who is always ready to hurl a lightning bolt because they think I certainly deserve it. In this instance, my son was not nice—he had been naughty. But I was not Santa Claus or Zeus, I was his father.

This doesn't mean that there is never a time to be direct and even critical. Jesus was often direct with his rebukes of certain religious people. But to the most vulnerable, his primary expressions were that of grace and mercy and love. When someone was already burdened with guilt and shame, he didn't pile on.

With my children, I found anger and vengeance to be easy, and mercy, love and forgiveness to be much harder. I had to be much more deliberate to administer what I was discovering as a much better way.

So, what is God like?

The Bible says, "The Son is the radiance of God's glory and the exact representation of his being."[1] Jesus is exactly like God and God is exactly like Jesus. When you see Jesus, you see God. Jesus is the face of the Trinity. If we want to understand the God of the Old Testament, we must interpret it through the lens of Jesus.

## Jesus is exactly like God and God is exactly like Jesus. When you see Jesus, you see God.

When we look at Jesus, we see the face of God. He turns conventional wisdom on its head with statements like: "Love your enemies;"[2] "Turn the other cheek;"[3] "Father forgive them."[4] This was as surprising to first-century Jews as it is to us today. As followers of Jesus we can trust the image that he gave us. This image of God's nature helps us to more responsibly evaluate the much older text of the Old Testament. His sermons, like the Sermon on Mount, give us guiding principles to apply to what we read and hear elsewhere. When we do this, we lose the need to force the Bible to do things it was never intended to do. In this way, we can give up some of the old notions we have about God, because Jesus clearly demonstrates what God is like. We do not have to demote the teachings of Jesus because we are trying to justify other passages. Jesus is the lens I need to use to view God by.

At this point in my life, it is enough for me to say the writers of the Old Testament recorded what they remember in the way that made sense to them. We do not have to force the Old Testament to be an accurate history book. We also do not have to lose any hope because we have less certainty about the details in certain stories—some are stories to teach lessons or amplify truth. They do not have to be accurate to be true. For me, this strengthens my faith. I can have more assurance of things that are certain like the testimony about Jesus. And, I have more trust in the unfolding revelation that is the story of God's people in the Bible. All of it makes sense through the lens of Jesus.

Raising children helped me understand what God is like. If God is like Santa Claus, then just like the mythical being, we lose interest when we do not get what we want, or when we do not feel like we can be good enough. If God is like Zeus, then God is ineffective at parenting us. He may get us to do things, but he'll never have our heart. But, if God is like Jesus then his mercy, love, and forgiveness can nurture a relationship that is fruitful. Like my children, we can all grow to be responsible humans who live productive, loving, and effective lives.

Now, I have an understanding of God that makes sense.

## FOR FURTHER THOUGHT

Reflect on the statements below. Don't overthink it, just let it flow. You can analyze it later.

1. What are your previous versions of God?

2. How are you beginning to see God?

3. What will it change about you to see God differently?

4. What are several words that summarize your thoughts about this chapter or what is a quote you would like to remember?

# THE LOVE OF GOD

I can remember the drive home from the hospital, the first time we fumbled through getting the car seat out of the car (with our son still in it). All we really knew at that point was we were bonded to our first-born son in a way that was hard to explain. We placed him in the middle of the room. This bond beckoned us to do whatever we could to nurture him. We knew that we loved him and not much else. I remember looking at Laura and thinking, *"Okay…what do we do now?"*

There was a controversy when our second child, Abbey, was born. We had wondered whether she was male or female especially since I was in charge of the "guess the sex and arrival time of the baby" contest. The doctor was being a little secretive with the reveal, Laura nearly had an episode with him and he revealed in that moment our baby was a girl. I remember thinking about this daughter and saying to myself, "No one in this world has ever made me so angry yet still invoked my love like you do!" I loved her even when she challenged me—later, I respected her for it.

When our third child, Lily, was little she had the most beautiful hair. One time she cut it all off in the middle of night—I was devasted. She has always taken the road less traveled, like the time she delivered a challenging rebuke as Valedictorian in high school instead of the normal pablum often parroted by high school students. I respected her for that, but I do not think I have ever loved and respected her more than these last few months as I have watched her meet every challenge of raising a child with developmental milestones from being born eight weeks early.

It goes without saying, I love my three children and have since they were born. I would go so far as to say that I loved them even before they were born. I would categorize this love as close to unconditional. There were times when I was frustrated with them. There were times when I doubted their love for me. They were normal teenagers and we went through all the struggles of parenting—but even when they were rebellious, it seemed to only draw me closer in my affections for them. I would say the only human who has loved them more unconditionally than me was Laura. Mothers seem to have the purest form of unconditional affection for their children; this love may even be stronger for their grandchildren.

### *The common denominator among all this is that, with very few exceptions and of those who were parents, they all loved their children.*

As a pastor, I have seen people in all manner of circumstances. I have seen drug-addicted and/or alcoholic parents. I have seen criminal children and rebellious actions of all kinds. I have witnessed people with means and people in poverty. I have seen all sorts of religious zealots and those that claim they hate God. I have seen people I admired and people I had a hard time understanding. The common denominator among all this is, with very few exceptions of those who were parents, they all loved their children. They may not have known how to parent effectively, making mistakes that led to perceptions of being bad parents; they may have scarred their children trying to be good parents; they may have been so frustrated with parenting that they wanted to give up. But, when I talked to each one personally, I could tell that there was nothing they loved more than their children. Most of them would even swear to be willing to die for their children.

One of my basic assumptions about God is that he is better than me. If he is not, then I have little need for him. Actually, I would still need him—I cannot breathe without his control, but his ineffectiveness would render him much less beneficial to me. If he is the same as me, or worse than me, he might even be a good friend, but he has no use to me as God. The scriptures were written by people who often portrayed God as a parent using the term Father. If God is Father and if he is love, then his love for his children must at least be better than the love I have for my children.

I know my children recognized my love at times. I would tell them I loved them, and they would say, "Yeah, but you have to love me because you are my dad." They knew I said that I loved them, and they even had some evidence that I did, but they were not sure about my motives. Did I love them just because or was it because I was somehow being forced into it by God or something else?

*We assume that God is doing something he does not want to do. If we assume that we are originally bad, and he cannot hardly stand to look at us, then it is almost like something or someone must talk him into loving us.*

We often have a similar view of God's love. We assume that God is doing something he does not want to do. If we assume that we are originally bad, and he cannot hardly stand to look at us, then it is almost like something or someone must talk him into loving us. It is like the child that no one wants on their sports team. Someone urges, "Come on, he's not that bad—I'll vouch for him. Give him a chance." If we would be honest, this is how we often feel about God's love. We make incorrect assumptions about how we feel at the time or what someone else told us is true.

We inadvertently think God loves some and not others. On one hand, we sing and preach about God being love and God loving everyone, but then we imagine God has favorites among those he loves. We imagine our denomination or belief system being righter and God favoring us a little more. We imagine that our nation of origin is better than most or all others and we label others as evil or sub-human so that we can secretly imagine God smiting them and approve various forms of violence.

During the civil war, this played out in a very real way. The United States arrived at a place in history where a mother could realistically have a child on both sides of the war; both sides of the battle might claim, "God is on our side and they are the enemy!" Imagine the mother's thoughts as the battle raged. Would her love be any stronger for either of her children? Now imagine that God is looking down on the whole world. He sees religious battles over belief systems that are all at least partially wrong. He sees countries that have all different sorts of problems and all different sorts of feelings toward one another based on religion or possessions or just plain ignorance. He sees all the people that die on the battlefield and all those likely to be killed by collateral damage. Just like the mother who saw two of her sons on the battlefield, God sees his children and he loves them all.

I have seen people live with the sad assumption that we give God a reason to love us. We imagine that we are somehow useful enough to be considered loveable to him. I admit I get trapped in this practice way too often. I was taught that I should do something for God because I have a duty. I unconsciously looked for approval that I did enough or did something significant enough that God would truly love me. It kept me with just enough shame to always need to be doing something for God. It is not that we doubt God loves us, we demote the intensity and permanence of his love.

## God loves us because of who he is not because of anything we do. He is obligated by his nature alone to love us.

God loves us because of who he is not because of anything we do. He is obligated by his nature alone to love us. We understand this partially because our nature as parents drives us to love at least somewhat unconditionally. We get a sense of this other-centered, self-giving love when we watch our children raise their children. We see them love without expectation and without restraint. Just like a mother's love is free and unencumbered, the love of the Father, Son, and Spirit flows from their love for each other freely to us. It is their nature to be especially fond of us because it is not only what they do—it is who they are!

My children had different responses to my love at different times in their lives. Sometimes they would accept it, then ignore what I did or said. Other times, they would actively rebel and resist my love. Still at times, they might pretend like it was not real. As a parent, my best move was to love them consistently even when they responded wrongly. Our response to God's love cannot change the nature of his affection for us, our response only changes our experience. Ted Dekker, in the *Forgotten Way*, says:

"What you believe about yourself never defines you; only what your Father believes about you truly defines you. Your beliefs and perceptions, however, do define the experience you have in this world."[1]

We are embraced by the love of God which cannot be separated from us. Our actions simply change the way his love feels, not the actual composition or expression of it. Repentance changes how we feel about God not how he feels about us. His love never changes, only the way we perceive it.

While I was still a young adult, I attended a small church for one Sunday. It was one of those "I should go to church" moments that turned out to be much more. As I sat in the pew after service, I remember being overwhelmed with how much God loved me. Even though I never returned to that church, the encounter there with my thoughts made a significant advance in my personal spiritual growth. My understanding of God's love had changed. I envisioned a love that could not be affected by any of the circumstances of my life. I somehow felt a love that could not be affected by me but could be accepted and appreciated by me. It was a reference point for the future. God...loves... me...period.

The moments when my children realized my love for them came more in subtlety than grand moments. It was a little look they gave or something in their hugs that told me they got it! As much as possible, my love for my children remained constant, but when their understanding of my love changed, then their experience also changed. God's affection for us is the most constant thing in the universe. May we come to know it more fully!

---

## FOR FURTHER THOUGHT

Reflect on the statements below. Don't overthink it, just let it flow. You can analyze it later.

1. What does it mean that God loves you?

2. When you think of the love of God, what are some things that cannot co-exist with love?

3. Look at 1 Corinthians 13. If God is love, then what other words or phrases describe God and what he does? For example, "God (love) *keeps no record of wrong*" (1 Cor. 13:5)? What does it say that God (love) does not do or is not?

4. What are several words that summarize your thoughts about this chapter or what is a quote you would like to remember?

# PRAYER AND CHALLENGES

As I write this, my youngest child will be twenty-two tomorrow. I remember when she was three years old and, for the first time, used a big girl word in a sentence. A couple of months ago, she gave birth to her son Jackson. He was born eight weeks premature by C-section due to complications. I watched as she anticipated this event, analyzed the challenges ahead, and then faced each milestone with great courage. I am so proud of her and her husband.

My daughter is a lot like me—she is stubborn and likes to debate/discuss issues. Of course, we know deep down we are not always right, but we seem to have the need to speak up for what we think is right and what we think needs to be said. Even though she is not afraid to speak her mind, during the entire experience I never heard her say, *"Why me?"* There were sometimes daily challenges she faced in the hospital, in addition to the normal grind of adjusting to and raising an infant. She endured and faced every challenge that came her way. I think this is a product of doing her homework and being prepared mentally--she realized anything can happen--and sometimes anything can happen to you!

Last night my wife and I were talking about prayer. We have moved beyond the superficial prayer life we used to have and are examining all avenues of prayer, thinking about prayer like we have never thought before. A great shift took place for me when I heard my pastor say, *"Prayer is not to get something from God, it is for us to be properly formed."* I later attended his prayer school where I learned about prayer liturgies and borrowing well-crafted prayers from the past, including prayers from Jesus and Saint Francis. I have been reading Julian of Norwich and getting familiar with the idea of simply being with God and considering my life as a prayer. It was in this context I discovered something about these two approaches to prayer that helped me understand God and prayer a little better.

I remember standing next to the incubator gazing down at my new grandson (Jackson) and I was overwhelmed. I had never been that close to such a small child. He was so small and had all kinds of tubes and sensors coming out from all around him. His skin was off color and he looked like he had been through a lot the past couple of days and indeed he had. His face looked somewhat bruised and it seemed like every spot that did not have a tube or sensor coming out of it had evidence of some past trauma. Some people tell me we are born evil, but after staring down at my grandson I could no longer believe it. When God created the first human in Genesis, he said, *"It was very good."* That is exactly what I thought when I saw Jackson, *"He has such a battle ahead of him, but it is all good!"'*

**I stood there next to the incubator that held my infant grandson in the chasm between life and death and in that moment of uncertainty, I cried.**

Looking across the incubator, I saw my baby girl. She always looks determined, but this was the first time I could see helplessness in her eyes. Lily's husband, Trevor, is a strong, determined young man but he also showed signs of confusion and concern. I do not blame either of them for being concerned or feeling helpless, I almost returned our first born because I had no idea what to do and I was facing nowhere near the challenges my daughter and her husband faced. I stood next to the incubator that held my infant grandson in the chasm between life and death and in that moment of uncertainty, I cried. As I struggled to accept the gravity of the moment, my mind wrestled with the concepts of acceptance, denial, and confusion. My thoughts were cloudy at best. Being in that place at that moment was somewhat like preparing to go down a road I had never traveled before.

In that moment I did not pray any eloquent prayers. I did not give any excellent advice to my children. I did not write any meaningful poems. I have always said we should have a ministry of presence; we should be there for people. In that moment when my daughter and her husband were fighting for the life of their newborn son with beautiful abandon, I was fighting the urge to run out of the room throwing medical equipment screaming, *"What the hell, God?!?"* I needed something more than platitudes or promises, I needed a partner who would stand with my family. I needed something or someone to tell me, not that this would be all better, but that we could somehow navigate it together.

*I needed a partner that would stand with my family. I needed something or someone to tell me, not that this would be all better, but that we could somehow navigate it together.*

Laura and I discussed, months later, what we both believe about prayer, how we prayed for Lily—what we think about our youngest daughter and what we imagine God thinks about us. I have already mentioned how we felt about our grandson from the instant we saw him. He is precious, he is good, he is loved, and he did not have to do anything to receive that. I simply gave it to him because he was all of these things! I have similar feelings toward our daughter. I have always loved her. I think she knows nothing she does can change that. There are some things my love provides like provision and compassion and forgiveness. But there are also things it does not include like judgement and the need to control. I found this especially true during the past few months. The things she needed and did not need became clearer—and when I did not get it, she told me!

*I did not hope that we would wake up tomorrow and have a different outcome. I did not pray for anything to change and I did not try to do something to make it change. I just stood in the hospital room and cried because that seemed like the appropriate thing to do.*

In the hospital that night, I did not feel the need to pray this would all go away. When I hear people say, "God is good", it is usually because something goes the way they imagined it would. There seems to be an unusually high expectation for persistent happiness in evangelical circles. Repeatedly, I have experienced situations in my life that did not go the way I wanted and instead turned out for the best anyway. These detours in life are often the path to maturity or growth, sometimes even the path to a better destination. So, no, I did not hope we would wake up tomorrow and have a different outcome. I did not pray for anything to change and I did not try to do something to make it change. I just stood in the hospital room and cried because it seemed like the appropriate thing to do.

I came to understand how God enters our situations. I now believe he, much like us, understands that what we most need is for him to be there, be present, and experience the pain with us. I think God sits with us, cries with us, walks with us, and reminds us when it is time to go out and get some real food! You see if God emptied out the hospitals, he would only be solving one of our problems. Physical healing has never been our biggest issue.

Laura always said I was a pushover for my two girls. I felt so helpless most of the time that when I got the opportunity, I jumped at the chance to do something for them. But, now that I can do more for them and have more resources, I find myself holding back often. I have learned to ask myself the question, "Is this the best thing I could do for them or is there something better?" I am learning my first inclination is usually wrong and asking this question forces me to stop and consider the alternatives. I suppose God always acts in my best interest whether I recognize it or not. If I am getting better at responding to crisis then God was always better all along!

I am still trying to sort through all the complex situations in everyday life and apply what I learn along the way. It seems like the responsible thing to do. The other night, I happened to watch the *Santa Clause* movie again and I remembered that I ruled out the Santa Claus version of god a few years ago. He doesn't make a list and check it twice to see if I have been naughty or nice. There is no way I could fully exhaust all the reasons for this in this book but suffice to say it is where I am now.

I do not believe in an angry and retributive god. I do not believe in the favorite uncle god that does whatever I want. These days I am focused on the God who comes to the hospital, stands next to my grandson's bed, and is with me when I cry. I can feel his hand holding mine, his arm around my shoulder. And when I turn and look at his face, I do not see the God of my youth. I see a Father with eyes full of love and a face stained with my tears, not because he is helpless or hopeless, but because I am his child and he is with me.

---

## FOR FURTHER THOUGHT

Reflect on the statements below. Don't overthink it, just let it flow. You can analyze it later.

1. Describe your ideas (past and present) of prayer.

2. Describe some recent challenges in your life. What do you want to say or illustrate about these situations? What feelings surface when you consider the challenges?

3. What are several words that summarize your thoughts about this chapter or what is a quote you would like to remember?

# GOD IS IN CONTROL?

My boss used to tell people I was his spiritual adviser. We had a pretty good relationship, but he probably did not like it when I went to work somewhere else. In the area of spiritual advice, the thing he remembered the most about me is one time when I told him, *"God is in Control."* Apparently, it helped him through some tough times when our company was struggling. The problem—it may not be true!

Some of the most frustrating and unrewarding times in my parenting life were when I tried to control the outcome. Controlling often seemed to make things worse and I eventually had to apologize for being a jerk and frustrating the ones I was trying to help. I remember helplessly muttering, "I am just trying to help" to one of my teenage children. Their reply was very simply, "You are not helping!" Most of the time they were right.

Controlling behavior is often rooted in some type of fear. Whether I was worried they were going to get hurt or I was worried my reputation was going to be diminished, the control never really helped much. If fact, it made it worse. I experienced this in church board rooms, in corporate offices, and especially in my home. We become afraid of something that might happen, we try to control the outcome, and usually it makes the situation worse. While it is comforting to think God is in control, it may be inaccurate to think he is controlling all our situations. While my views of control and my methods of control are inherently flawed, I am moving away from a view of a controlling God.

What are some better ways to view God than controlling?

I think we could safely say God *inspires* us. Inspiration is better than control or manipulation. Sometimes, we can inspire people by just being who we are. Certainly, God inspires us by the example of Jesus and the reality of his being. But God also has apparently called people to various journeys of faith with no definite promise of outcome except presence—*"I will be with you."*[1]

My children did not use a checkbook in their teen years. To me, this was a sure sign they were going to end in financial ruin. They resisted, we argued, and they went back to doing it their own way. Later, I discovered one of the best ways to inspire my children was to set an example for them. So, Laura and I tried to set an example and hoped it would inspire them. The other day, I observed that all three of them manage money better than we did at their age. They rarely need any help with money issues.

> **God sometimes allows us to experience some things because, like a good parent, he knows we are going to resist him anyway.**

I think God also *comforts* us instead of controlling our outcomes. Early on in my children's lives, I used to try to catch them before they fell. After the first toddler, I learned to say, "That is going to hurt," and let them experience a certain amount of pain. In a similar way, God sometimes allows us to experience some things because, like a good parent, he knows we are going to resist him anyway. He is always there to comfort when we skin our knees and he knows we will not be as likely to do that again.

What we need most is someone who will enter our story, especially after we have messed up, and simply sit with us in it. What we do not need is to succeed at everything we do. When parents orchestrate their children's circumstances, they produce immature adults, choosing comfort over control. Similarly, I think we develop spiritually, emotionally, and intellectually when challenges are allowed into our lives.

**When parents orchestrate their children's circumstances, they produce immature adults. Comfort is way better than control.**

When our children first learned to walk, they were always in a hurry to get somewhere and explore new things. They would get about ten feet ahead of us, stop, and turn around to see if we were still there. As a parent, my children need to know I am with them. Progressively, they needed me to control less and less. This made them feel secure, not that I was doing everything for them, but that I was always "there."

My children used to get tired of me saying, "Team Forehand." But, when they were in college and broke, they appreciated it a little more when they needed money. I changed it up to say, "We are in this together." I think they like that a lot better. They know I am for them. I think this is a better description of God—he is for us. It seems to make more sense than he is in control of us.

I do not want to discuss my children's mistakes. Even though they were pretty good, they did make a few. Some of them they may not know that we know—but this is okay too. We realized our children would make mistakes. We tried to prepare ahead of time. I did not encourage them to make mistakes, but they knew if they did, they were still loved, and they would learn something from the experience. I also told them, no matter what they did I would always love them. This seemed more productive than trying to keep them from making mistakes. God could keep me from making mistakes, but instead he gives me the freedom to fail. Then afterward he comes, like the prodigal's father, and restores me.

For my children and for myself, God is *not* in control, or at least he doesn't choose to control me and my situations. I'm glad there are cosmic and consistent things like gravity and planetary alignment that God orchestrates. I can still admit that this order to the universe is important, but not the same as controlling me and my situations. If I am honest with myself, I can see the request for an outside force to be in control of my life is an unnecessary request. Control is not really what I need, my children do not need me to control them, and it is certainly not what I need from God. I need inspiration—I need comfort—I need encouragement. I need his love. It is about what's best for us not just what we want at the time.

God is not in control because God is love and his love allows me to grow and mature, to be a better father to my children, to lead my family better than fear ever could.

---

## FOR FURTHER THOUGHT

Reflect on the statements below. Don't overthink it, just let it flow. You can analyze it later.

1. What things do you think God controls?

2. What things do you falsely assume God should "fix" or "control" in your life?

3. What kinds of things *inspire* you? How might God be involved in that?

4. What brings you *comfort*? How might God be involved in that?

5. What sorts of things *encourage you?* How might God be involved in that?

6. What are several words that summarize your thoughts about this chapter or what is a quote you would like to remember?

# RELIGION AND PRACTICE

"Human beings form religions around the things that matter to them and the fears that drive them toward certainty. For many, Christianity has become a religion."

**—WM. PAUL YOUNG**[1]

The old wisdom used to be, "Do not ever talk about religion and politics." For my mother and I, that would be good advice. But my children are different. For whatever reason, they have a lot to say about religion and politics. Since I was a pastor, we tried to avoid talking about religious things in our home (they got plenty of exposure in church and my wife and I thought they did not want to talk about it at home). That was probably a good move, but it did not stop my children from forming very strong opinions about religion and politics. Today, I consider my three children very astute in both arenas and I often discretely solicit advice from them.

Earlier in their lives, I was less confident about having political or religious discussions with them. After all, that was how I was raised—nothing good can come of it. My cousin argued with my grandpa Joe and it seemed like a waste of time. Despite all my hang ups, I approached my daughter one day and asked her, "How do you really feel about church?" She responded, "I'd rather be on a mountain thinking about God than be in church thinking about a mountain." Some have taken this further, from a preference for rejecting religion outright to opting for a more private experience. We certainly have had tension in our religious history. My daughter's comment caused me to examine some things.

A common phrase today is, "Jesus did not come to start a religion." Some of my friends would respond, "He did not start a religion because he already had one—he was a Jew and he practiced Judaism." Was Jesus religious because of his parents or because he was God? Do we need religion? Is it required? Some of my wiser friends would say, "Yes, because it helps us be properly formed." But even they would admit the answer is more complicated.

> ### Religion seems to satisfy a basic longing that all of us have. To me, religion had always been about finding a road to God, reestablishing a relationship.

Religion seems to satisfy a basic longing all of us have. To me, religion had always been about finding a road to God, reestablishing a relationship. Since the time of Jesus and the Samaritan woman, we associate our faith with a place or an organization. This always confuses the issue. Maybe it is not so much about finding a road to God as it is opening a path for him to reach us. Or if you prefer, making space, or just being open.

For me, it helps tremendously to not use the word church or religion, these are currently trigger words for my wife and me. I prefer the word practice. A couple of times, in the Gospel of Luke, Jesus is led by his *ethos* (his custom, his habit). If we are not careful, we can use this understanding to legalize a pre-scribed way to worship and pray and interact with God. I believe we must see both sides of the coin. Others have passed faith onto us and we borrow those customs and traditions that help form us. But, sometimes, we also need to adopt new practices that help us on the journey. Jesus practiced the religion of his ances-tors, but he also reserved the right to exercise "his" practice. If it was not a little unorthodox, then why did it upset people at the time? He went to the temple but also went out to the garden. I feel the same about meditation and yoga—it is not really about what I like, it is about what is effective. As God, Jesus shows us what pleases God. But, as a human, he also showed us that time, location, situation and station in life can all affect the practice.

**Others have passed faith onto us and we borrow those customs and traditions that help form us. But, sometimes, we also need to adopt new practices that help us on the journey.**

I have learned recently my practice needs to celebrate pres-ence. I am somewhat of a task-oriented person. I like to accom-plish things and know what my mission is so I can accomplish it effectively. Through things like centering prayer, I am discov-ering the value of being present. Centering prayer is a practice where I sit, often with a word, and just celebrate the fact that I am here—I am breathing—I am enough—I am present. But I also celebrate the fact that God is here. I am learning I do not need to always ask for something or even to expect anything. When one of my daughters rode with me in the car, she always talked non-stop. When the other rode with me, we sometimes did not talk much at all. My son was a combination of the two.

It is possible and appropriate to be together and be at peace. I am truly discovering the truth behind an old phrase we used to say in church, "It is good to be together."

I was recently unemployed for the first time in twenty-five years. I decided to make the most of it and get up early to just sit, meditate, pray and read. When I was quiet and still, one of the most common emotions or qualities that arose in me was appreciation. Appreciation for God—appreciation of myself—and, surprisingly, an appreciation of others. Appreciate means "to recognize the full worth of" or "raise in value." When I recognize the true worth of things that matter, I cannot help but draw closer to God. When my children learn to appreciate the things I value, and vice versa, we draw closer. Things like adoration, appreciation, and thanksgiving are gifts that keep on giving.

As a pastor, I used to worry a lot when I went to church. I was a bit of a rebel, but mostly I wanted the ministry leaders who checked in on me to approve of what I was doing. I also found that I needed feedback from the congregation and my wife on a regular basis. Was I doing things in the right way? I was pained when they started to disapprove of certain things. When I changed my practice, there were a few people who told me I was on a slippery slope for doing such things as yoga or meditation. Even if I called it centering prayer, it was still a little too "catholic" for some.

### Trying harder often made it worse. This can also be true of church and religion.

I worried about my relationship with my children because, to be honest, we did not have the best practices. We did not talk enough, and when we did, it was not very genuine or honest. We desired to be closer, but it did not always happen, and we would leave frustrated. Trying harder often made it worse. This can also be true of church and religion. I know it to be true of my relationship with God. Much like my relationship with my children, I must practice the things that make the relationship effective.

I feel like things are changing for me. I do not know if my practices are better, but they seem more authentic. I find myself talking about them more with my children and others. I experience more of a presence in my practices and this also feels more authentic. As my practice becomes more authentic, I feel more appreciation and thankfulness, not just for what is now but what has come before this time to prepare the way for me to be where I am. And, with conversation, there usually comes more honesty.

My practice is anything but fixed—it seems to change slightly every day and is a mixture of what was handed down to me and what I am discovering. My practice is contemplative, and it is active; it is a mixture of liturgy and mysticism (experience), mystery and paradox. My practice is more of a journey than anything else.

The best part of my current practice is being able to talk about it with my children. I no longer have to defend it; it is authentic and not designed for anyone else. I do not regret where I have been (because it formed me), but I am excited about where I am going.

I pray you will find your practice!

## FOR FURTHER THOUGHT

Reflect on the statements below. Don't overthink it, just let it flow. You can analyze it later.

1. Describe or illustrate your current practices.

2. What are some new practices that you want to incorporate?

3. What are some barriers to your practices?

4. Make a list of what characterizes true religion and false religion.

5. What are several words that summarize your thoughts about this chapter or what is a quote you would like to remember?

# CELEBRATING

Have you ever watched a child learn how to ride a bicycle? John McMurray describes the time when he and his wife taught their son how to ride a bicycle, it is a beautiful description of what happens when the child finds the "sweet spot" and experiences joy and freedom:

> "Then, all of a sudden…he got it. He found the sweet spot with his balance, and he was off…Terri and I looked at each other and saw the same grin on our faces. 'Way to go, Superman!' Terri exclaimed as high fives were profusely exchanged."[1]

Reading this depiction brought back all kinds of memories I have with my children. Memories of when they first walked or when they first spoke coherently, when they learned to drive, when they learned to read, when I walked my daughters down the aisle and when they gave birth to their own children, when they articulated their beliefs and passions. I could go on. The commonality in all these experiences is that they were all group experiences. The entire family was involved, we were near each other, intently interested in what the other was doing, cheering for the other in the relationship, inviting them in some way to experience what we already knew. We call it a "team," but it is far greater. This feeling of oneness goes deeper than any sports team could ever feel for each other.

The oneness my family periodically experienced is a lot like what I am coming to understand about the Trinity—the Father, Son and Spirit. Some theologians refer to this relationship as the *perichoresis*. This "divine dance" of self-giving, other-centered love is what Baxter Krueger so eloquently describes in his book, *Across All Worlds: Jesus Inside Our Darkness.*

"Within the being of God there is relationship – three persons united in mutual love and communion without the loss of personal distinctness. The relationship of the Father, Son and Spirit is a rich and unclouded fellowship that is so deep and true, so open and close, and fired by such pure love, that we are driven with historic Christianity to say they are one. Anything less than 'one' betrays the very closeness of their relationship. Yet the Father does not become the Son or the Spirit and the Son and the Spirit do not become one another or the Father. This is a relationship of oneness, yet not absorption. This is a relationship of thorough ongoing communion in mutual self-giving love, in which the Father, Son and Spirit have such a profound freedom to know and be known that they share things together without losing themselves in enmeshment."[2]

## We were created from relationship for relationship, invited to experience this other-centered, self-giving love not only with God but also with each other.

The Father, Son and Spirit were not lonely or in need when they created man—they were already in a relationship. We were created from relationship for relationship, invited to experience this other-centered, self-giving love not only with God but also with each other. Sometimes this feels very real from one moment to the next. I feel this the strongest when I am with my family. Being with my family nurtures this sense of genuine love, relationship, and celebration. We celebrated as a family with each child when they reached a milestone. It was pure love—it seemed like what life should be like!

When I was studying spiritual leadership coaching, a peer of mine asked me a simple question. She said, *"Karl, how do you celebrate?"* That question stunned me. I did not have an answer. I started to tear up because I was sensing what the answer might be, and I did not like it. I was a pastor at the time and should have had a better answer. All I could say was, *"I am not sure if I know how."* Sure, several times in my life I sort of celebrated with my family, but for the most part my ability to celebrate had become mired down in too many things.

Celebration was stifled by the transactional nature of pop Christianity. Even though I talked about my faith as a relationship, it often resembled more of a contract or transaction. I was focused on my calling and what I did for Jesus more than the relationship I had with Him. I preached about joy and peace but had little of either.

I was focused on my duty and what I believed more than my relationship with the one I believed in. I remember bragging about the fact that I spent eight to ten hours, on average, preparing for a sermon. To be honest, there was some payback for me. I would make discoveries during that time that brought excitement and fulfillment, then, I would share those discoveries with the congregation and revel in the fact that it blessed or challenged them. This is not necessarily bad, but I wonder what would have happened if one Sunday I would have said, "This week, I just spent my preparation time sitting with Jesus and celebrating our relationship." I suspect that would be okay for one or two Sundays, but not much more.

Too often I did not treat my relationship with the Trinity like a relationship. I did not celebrate much since I was quickly onto the next task after finding a little success. At times, it was more like a business arrangement than a relationship. We were bound more by the commandments or the commission than what Paul described as our debt of love.

When my children took their first step or rode their first bike, Laura and I did not tell them, "Now that you can talk, your primary purpose is to tell me how grateful you are for teaching you this new skill." Being thankful is a good thing, but it is not the primary thing you do in a relationship. Laura and I did not say, "Now that you can ride a bicycle, you should be busy going to all the other children in the neighborhood to tell them about your parents." Sharing what we know is a good thing, but is it the primary reason we learned to ride the bicycle? This is a big one for me—my friends call me a crusader, too busy doing what I understand to be my mission or duty to the Kingdom instead of focusing on the fellowship and love of the Trinity. Fear drives me to do the unusual things I do.

### I did not have time or the inclination to experience joy or peace—I did not feel right celebrating!

I had a hard time celebrating because I saw God as distant, transactional—he saved me, commissioned me and was expecting great things of me. I did not have time or the inclination to experience joy or peace—I did not feel right celebrating! Celebrating was embarrassing, excessive, and felt unnecessary. But in a true relationship—when there is other-centered, self-giving love for each other, encouraging each other, when we have nothing but hope, love, understanding, and patience— joy and celebration flow naturally. This celebration of love is the main ingredient in worship and feels like the "spirit and truth" worship that Jesus talked about.

I am learning to celebrate, and yet, in learning to celebrate I found I did not have to learn to celebrate. Celebration is a natural outpouring of the relationship I have with God. The Father, Son and Spirit were celebrating with me just like I celebrated with my children.

It's more about flowing into the relationship that is flowing out to me. It's a little like learning to ride a bicycle and hitting the "sweet spot." It's like the first time I ran without falling. It's like finally letting go and letting it flow through me. Celebration is a little different for everyone and a little different for various situations. Take some time to explore it below.

It's time to join in the dance!

## FOR FURTHER THOUGHT

Reflect on the statements below. Don't overthink it, just let it flow. You can analyze it later.

1. What does it feel like or look like when you celebrate?

2. Describe the Trinity?

   • What are the characteristics of that relationship?

   • What is your relationship (where are you?) in the picture?

3. Contemplate any barriers that keep you from celebrating.

4. What are several words that summarize your thoughts about this chapter or what is a quote you would like to remember?

# THE BIBLE

As I walked up to the pulpit lectern at the fundamentalist Bible church where I was the pastor, each time I would say out loud, *"I have nothing of value to say that is not already written in this book."* Looking back now, I am saddened because I had made Scripture—this life-giving, breathing, living thing—an idol. Jesus often quoted the Old Testament, but he never held out Scripture as an idol to be placed above all other things. He said things like, "You have heard it said...But, I say to you..." This happened several times in the Sermon on the Mount alone. He was quoting Hebrew Scripture (the only Scripture they had) and changing it. At other times, he seemed to ignore or disobey what others believed Scripture prescribed as law. Christians, especially protestants, started to idolize Scripture after the Reformation with the pronouncement, "Sola Scriptura" (Scripture Alone). Sadly, I too was caught up in this thought process for a long time.

My children and their friends taught me to look at things differently. I noticed these young people discovering inconsistencies and posing magnificent questions. I enjoyed answering emails from students and other people who were investigating the Bible, but at some point, I grew weary of justifying things like genocide and slavery and rules/laws that did not make any sense. Slowly, I began to wonder, "What if I am wrong?"

What if this book is something more than a rigid book of rules? What if it is a record of the people of God as they progressed through their understanding of God, the world, and each other? What if, dare I say, the Bible contains errors and inconsistencies that are understandable but not what I was taught dogmatically?

**For Christians, the focus should be primarily on Jesus Christ. After all, we were first labeled as "little Christ's" in the New Testament.**

Over the years as I allowed more things to become a question mark instead of a statement, the answers became clearer. I began to see a Christlike God who is loving, merciful, and full of grace. I understood what he said about not coming to judge the world, I saw his compassion and felt his love for the whole world. I read several authors like Peter Enns, Keith Giles and Brad Jersak who encouraged me to interpret the Bible through the lens of Jesus. Jesus' words and actions became the starting pointing for understanding what the Bible says, and sometimes, what it did not. Through my pastor, Brian Zahnd, I came to understand Christianity as a tree and the Bible as the soil out of which it grows. Both need each other, but they are separate and different. And, by the way, we do not need to idolize either one of them. For Christians, the focus should be primarily on Jesus Christ. After all, we were first labeled as "little Christ's" in the New Testament.

Taking the Bible literally and claiming that it is inerrant requires some prerequisites. One of those prerequisites is to consider how the Bible came together. In the year 325 A. D., multiple councils met to formalize the Scriptures to include both the Hebrew Scriptures and some 1st Century writings in one coherent volume or canon. This coincides with Constantine's action to unite the church with Empire and his desire to have 50 copies of a standard canon in the Church of Constantinople around 331 A.D. By the 5th century, a series of councils had met and agreed on the Canon of Scripture. Questions still lingered for me though and I wondered, "How do I, we, know that they got it right?"

A great example of my struggle with this is found in interpreting 2 Kings 1 (Old Testament for those following along in their Bibles). Moab rebels against Israel, Ahaziah has an accident and wants to know if he will recover. So, he sends messengers to ask the god of Ekron to make the call. Apparently, this upsets the angel of the Lord who sends the prophet Elijah to ask him, "Is it because there is no God in Israel that you are going to inquire of Baal-Zebub, the god of Ekron?" The angel adds, "You shall surely die." God seems to go out of his way here just because he did not get consulted.

After Elijah delivers the message, the king sends a captain and fifty men to invite Elijah to come visit with these words: "O man of God, the king says, 'Come down.'" Apparently, that is the wrong thing to say to a prophet because he responds, "If I am a man of God, let fire come down from heaven and consume you and your fifty." And, according to the account, fire came down and consumed them. Overreact much? The scene is repeated for the second squad of fifty, but narrowly avoided in the third regiment because the third captain begs for his life. His men are spared, and the angel instructs Elijah to take the time to deliver the message that the king is going to die because he ignored God.

I do not know about you, but this leaves me with a few questions. Is this story true? If it is literally accurate, is it what we are supposed to do? And, more importantly, is this an accurate representation of what God is like?

> **Jesus stressed that God does not do drone strikes on people just because they ignore or offend him.**

If only we could find an example in the Bible that would clear this up. For those of you following along, let's turn to Luke 9 (New Testament) where James and John are traveling with Jesus. Jesus and his disciples happen upon a village of Samaritans who refuse to provide traveling accommodations to Jesus and his group. James and John wondered (out loud apparently), "Lord, do You want us to command fire to come down from heaven and consume them?" This was a great teaching moment for the disciples. In their minds, this is what God does when someone disrespects him—it is what he did to the King of Israel in the Moabite story above. Jesus brings clarity with a simple statement, "You do not know what kind of spirit you are, for the Son of Man (Jesus) did not come to destroy men's lives, but to save them." Jesus stressed that God does not do drone strikes on people just because they ignore or offend him. His purpose was to save lives, and apparently, that included physical ones. How then are we left to interpret the story from the Old Testament of Moab, the King, and Elijah?

One of the verses most often quoted concerning Scripture is part of a letter Paul wrote to Timothy. He tells Timothy that Scripture is "inspired." He continues and tells him that is also "useful" or "profitable" for several things. Without going into detail, I would say that just because something is inspired by God does not necessarily make it infallible. I have often been inspired, but rarely am I without error. If you see the Bible in a more literal way, you would probably argue for different kinds of inspiration. The evidence I see doesn't point to the fact that Jesus or Paul thought this inspiration meant anything like infallibility as Jesus and Paul often interpreted Hebrew Scriptures in interesting ways that do not point to inerrancy. I would also stress that since Scripture is inspired, it absolutely is useful (profitable) for many things.

When I look at Scripture through the lens of Jesus, I see a graceful, merciful, compassionate God; I also understand the purpose of the Bible better. It is "useful," as it says, but I am no longer inclined to treat it as a rule book or accurate historical record. It is the soil which nurtures the tree of Christianity. It is a record of God's people in all their immaturity and lack of understanding. It was recorded by people that were certainly inspired, but not infallible.

To some extent, my theology classes looked at how the Bible was translated. I do not really have the inclination to dive into that currently. But, suffice to say, I still have doubts that every single word of our current Bible made it through multiple translations and copies without some errors occurring. Understanding that does not deter my faith—it kind of strengthens it. It makes me believe a little less in the Bible and a little more in the Word of God (Jesus). I am okay with that.

Some of my friends think I will not need the Bible if I do not take it so literally. I think the healthiest thing to say is that I still have questions and I think it is okay to keep discovering truth. Sometimes that comes outside the Bible, sometimes it comes through the words written there, often, it is a combination of both. My understanding of the Bible is progressively changing as my understanding of God changes.

Through my children, and others on this journey, I have discovered that I often have something of value to say outside of what I quote from the canon of Scripture. Last Sunday I preached for the first time in over a year. As I walked to the pulpit, I carried my Bible with confidence. But I did not say, "I have nothing of value to say outside of this book." I did open my Bible—I did quote from two passages. My pastor's words seem to come alive in me. The Bible was a soil out of which my sermon grew, but it was not an idol to be worshipped. It was very much a part of the story, but I also had valuable things to share from my experiences with my children and grandchildren. It was all good—it was all useful—and people were blessed not because I gave them some platitude or absolute statement, but that maybe for the first time, I used the Scriptures a little more like Jesus did. And that is what I see my journey to be.

I am not on a journey to prove the Bible. I am on a journey to discover Jesus!

---

## FOR FURTHER THOUGHT

Reflect on the statements below. Don't overthink it, just let it flow. You can analyze it later.

1. Consider your views (past and present) of the Bible.

   • How does it relate to God?

- What is the purpose and position of the Bible in your life?

- What should we say about the Bible? Is it literal, accurate, inerrant?

- Why do some people call it the "Word of God?"

2. What are several words that summarize your thoughts about this chapter or what is a quote you would like to remember?

# THE TEA SHOP

"Every day God invites us on the same kind of adventure. It is not a trip where He sends us a rigid itinerary, He simply invites us. God asks what it is He's made us to love, what it is that captures our attention, what feeds that deep indescribable need of our souls to experience the richness of the world He made. And then, leaning over us, He whispers, 'Let's go do that together.'"[1]

**—BOB GOFF**

This past summer, we went to visit my son in Taiwan where he teaches English. We scheduled some time to go to the Southern section of the island. This part of Taiwan is less densely populated and offered us the promise of an adventure. I was hungry for getting off the main path and experiencing the beauty of Taiwan. As I stated before, I was trying to learn to express this part of my inner child. I wanted to have fun—I wanted to celebrate—I wanted adventure.

Part of this journey involved renting scooters to explore the beautiful area of Taroko Gorge National Park. As we were getting comfortable with the scooters and heading out to the gorge, I noticed I was accelerating instead of stopping at a traffic light. I hit the brakes, but I hit the wrong brake. Instantly, I found myself airborne and heading for the pavement just beyond the front of my rented scooter. I still have the scars from the places that contacted the street. I would have rolled or something cool like that, but I did not have time. I was not badly injured, but it threw us for a loop that day. We had to re-plan our trip and I wondered if I had ruined the whole excursion.

**_Why could I not admit that I am a little old to be running around on scooters and looking for adventure? We could just as easily have been sitting on a beach instead._**

Waves of emotion washed over me. In addition to the pain and inconvenience of having to dress wounds for the rest of the trip, I felt kind of foolish for wanting to have an adventure. Why could I not admit that I am a little old to be running around on scooters and looking for adventure? We could just as easily have been sitting on a beach instead. Those kinds of thoughts are what you think when you are sitting at a noodle shop in pain from the adventure and the immediate future of the trip is in question. Thoughts of a more tragic accident also ran through my mind, but that is probably a much longer discussion.

A few days later, we traveled back North. If I would not have wrecked my scooter, we might have still been down in the Southern part of Taiwan that day. My unfortunate accident caused us to have a couple of extra days to venture around in the more populated Northern region. One night, as our host Tanya was dropping us off at the hotel after supper, Laura decided to ask one last question, "Where could we pick up a teapot?" Laura and I had wanted to find one to commemorate the visit and give to our daughters but had been unable to take the time to do so. I had been a little too busy trying to adjust after the scooter incident.

Tanya told us to jump in her vehicle and we headed off into the night. The streets which were usually crowded full of scooters and pedestrians during the day were calmer. At night, 10PM to be exact, only a small swarm of scooters surrounded us at each stop light. Tanya made her way confidently to the specific shop she had in mind. As we pulled up in front of what looked like an old English shop from the outside, dimly lit and slightly unkept, she said, "This is it." It was approximately 12 feet deep and probably fifty feet long. Not where I expected to find the tea pot to take home to my daughters.

At this point, I caught a glance of my son, Jordan (otherwise known as J.D.). When I was injured, he successfully navigated the clinics on the South end of the island to get me some very capable, inexpensive treatment for my wounds. This included communicating with the Mandarin speaking Taiwanese doctors and nurses and even comforting me in my distress. He was playing the part of the father for me when I felt helpless. I was glad he was along on the journey with me. I am glad for my son; he is my best friend. In a way, he was directly showing me the heart of the Father on this trip.

As Laura and I walked through the front door of the tea shop, I went into consumer mode. Being slightly uncomfortable, I zeroed in on the mission of finding the tea pots. A tea table, common to many shops in the area, was the focal point of the room. A thick large slice of a tree, the table was heavily varnished, mostly covered with various articles too numerous to differentiate. Even as the shelves of the room were a sea of eclectic items, the table was even more so, covered in a plethora of colors, shapes, and sizes and, at first glance, a bunch of random stuff.

I did not see the shop owner when I entered the room. It soon became apparent that he was the center of attention. Several locals were gathered around and focused on him. He wore very modern clothes—a pair of slacks and a pullover shirt, comfortable shoes for being on your feet all day long. His face showed some signs of his actual age, but his body was like that of a teenager. He moved with ease and later demonstrated just how agile and flexible he was. Tonya told us about his life progressing from an orphan to a shop owner. It was inspiring although he did not seem to be living in the past. He was most definitely in the present.

Tanya introduced us and told those in the shop that we were looking for a teapot. They were speaking Mandarin and probably in the Taiwanese dialect. I had tried to learn some of the language, but I failed miserably and most of the locals wanted to practice their English on me anyway.

We were already busy looking for a teapot and my eyes were quickly glazing over from the sheer amount of merchandise in the tiny space. The shop owner and the locals got a feel for what we were interested in and found several that matched what we had in mind. After we settled on a couple of teapots we were interested in, the man behind the table invited us to have tea with him. I had given up caffeine a couple of years ago, but I sensed this was going to be an experience—so, I agreed. Laura and I sat down with our son, Jordan, and our host Tanya, to have a cup of tea.

I sat directly across from the unnamed man in the mysterious tea shop and began to have tea with him. Having tea for some cultures is more of a ceremony, a process. This was not just preparing a drink for a guest. He had a specific ritual that seemed to be a combination of precision and artistic flow. I would later discover this was how he did most everything. I have discovered, that once this process begins, it continues until something else happens to shift the focus. He would heat the water in some sort of modern contraption and then pour it over tea leaves in the tiny decorated pot. The individual teas seemed to have significance and required some approval and feedback, but as I mentioned, I was not interpreting everything correctly at this point. I always describe the smell of Taiwan as unique—it is not good or bad—it just is. In the tea shop, the smells of the tea seemed to overcome the smell of the streets and somehow made us feel something slightly different. A bit of peace and tranquility—this made me only a little bit uneasy.

Along with the constant supply of tea, the man began to share about his *ethos,* his practice. Tanya told us he was explaining his specific yoga practice he learned from someone else. I am still not sure what it was—like most of the evening, nothing had a label. He stood on a stump and showed us how flexible and agile he was. One thing I knew for sure—he felt it contributed to his youth and flexibility. This seemed to require an "ooh" and an "ahh" from me, so that was what I did. He was 60 years old but seemed to have the dexterity of a much younger man. I am always trying to dissect and figure things out. How does this work? How did he do that? I desperately wanted him to give me a book or DVD about this practice, but it was obvious that was not going to happen. Like the teapots, I wanted to bring back souvenirs of our time in beautiful Taiwan and I was searching for things that would make my life work better. I did not know yet all that I would take home from this shop, but I was sensing it was something good!

Before our trip, Laura and I had begun a journey of eating only plant-based foods. We did it mostly for health reasons although later, we also became concerned about the treatment of animals and the environment. Up to that point in the trip, the highlight so far had been a vegetarian meal at a Buddhist restaurant where we were privileged to eat. They were so kind and so helpful, and the food was so good. In the tea shop, my son and Tanya told the man that we were plant-based. He promptly invited us to share his supper with him as both he and his wife were, in fact, plant-based also. Most likely they were vegetarians, and not full vegans, but the distinction did not seem to matter at the time. Even as he invited us to eat with him, I thought, "Ha! This is what usually happens when I go to the store--we watch a guy tell stories and then eat dinner with him!" Briefly, I wondered if this would be the part of the story where the Americans were all poisoned and the Taiwanese lived happily ever after. I trusted Tanya though and we all agreed that even though it was late, and we had already eaten, we would stay for supper.

As we were finishing dinner, Tanya helped negotiate a price for the teapots. She assured us it was a bargain. Without announcement, he immediately began to macramé a little twine rope braid onto the teapots. It was a connector from the handle to the lid to keep it from getting lost. I do not know if he did this for every customer, but it made me feel special. As he did this, he would occasionally spring up, then dart to some area of the shop and return with something in his hand. He moved effortlessly like a teenager full of life and excitement.

His supper was filling, delicious, and added another layer to the trip, yet he still brought us peanuts and then sunflower seeds afterwards. Again, I do not know why. I got the sense he was trying to make us happy. It was working! I was beginning to feel a sense of connection with our host and satisfaction with making the decision to venture out into the night. This was an adventure I was going to be glad that I embarked upon. Then, he came back with a bottle.

Something in the way the guy's friend reacted made me think this was a special deal. I think it was the tone of his voice when he said with enthusiasm, "That is a new bottle!" Tanya quickly explained that the bottle contained alcohol usually not given to foreigners. The bottle had a colorful label with Chinese characters. Inside, the liquid was clear and seemed unmenacing on the surface. This did not happen every day! The thought quickly raced through my mind about dying right there in the tea shop from alcohol poisoning. *My God, what would Laura tell the police? That I was poisoned by a young but old, very flexible man with no name who makes good tea?*

The bottle looked like it held grain alcohol. If you have ever had moonshine—that is about the size of it. Holy rice wine Batman! That was strong! Someone mentioned something about taste, but I could not feel anything in my mouth. I noticed he was beginning to fiddle with something else. This time it was his characters. If you do not know, characters are how Chinese communicate visually. They are complex and usually depict a word or phrase instead of just one letter.

**He seemed compelled to make me happy—whatever it took.**

He gave us some business cards with characters on them, then a sheet of graph paper with some characters he had written. Even Tonya was not much help understanding this writing. Although she is very wise and understands various cultures including the United States, she said something like "I understand it, but it is very hard to explain." When he saw that we appreciated the characters, he began writing something for me. By this time, I was simply feeling very touched. He seemed compelled to make me happy—whatever it took. This was beyond customer service—I think he genuinely wanted to make people feel joy. I do not know if he was focusing his attention on me, but that is what it felt like.

The shop owner was one of those people that others are attracted to, but I experienced him as one of the most genuine people I have encountered in a long time. He had time for me, he was interested in me, and he took the time to make me happy!

There are probably a dozen lessons I learned that night, but I want to stew on them for a while. I walked out of the tea shop saying, *"What just happened?"*, and have been thinking about my experience there ever since. I was hoping for an adventure and was astonished I found it at a tiny little tea shop with no name in an interesting little man who could not speak my language.

I hope I can learn to slow down and be the kind of person I witnessed that night! I want to take time to love people instead of just serving myself. I hope I can find the time to be present with people and share my food with them. Maybe I can remember to say something kind to the next service industry employee I encounter.

I imagine Jesus to be a lot like the man with no name. I cannot wait to visit him the next time I travel to Taiwan.

## FOR FURTHER THOUGHT

Reflect on the statements below. Don't overthink it, just let it flow. You can analyze it later.

1. Have you ever had an experience like the Tea Shop?

   • What did it teach you about yourself?

   • What did it teach you about God?

2. What does it mean be more *present?*

3. Consider the fact that the present is the only time you can live in.

4. What are several words that summarize your thoughts about this chapter or what is a quote you would like to remember?

## Section 2

# REFLECTIONS

# AH, THE MILLENNIALS

I can remember the moment I began to realize I was learning from my children. The amount of struggle and experience up to that point in my life had prepared me to be ready to learn from my children and their friends. But this did not happen the way I thought it would. As I look around the room, I see others of my generation unwilling to listen and engage with each other leaving themselves alienated.

I know it is popular to criticize the millennials. This seems to be a part of my human nature when I encounter something different—I learned it was fight or flight after all. When my children were young, I used to see all the similarities between us, they were the same as me! My son had the same facial features, my daughters gladly held my wife's beauty within them instead of my own. I felt a sense of pride in that, but I am glad they're turning out to be different than me. I think it is a positive quality of the next generation that they're different than my own, maybe they'll get us out of some of the messes we have made.

Let me explain.

One day, my daughter told me, "Dad, do not get your validation from others!" Where did she ever get that idea from? I would never...pshhh...I cannot imagine...absurd! That statement hit me like a brick to the face, it was hard to admit she might have been right. Now to be fair, I used to get most of my self-worth from what people said about me. I had to be the best preacher, husband, father, business man, saver, scripture reader, etc. It was as if my entire life was under a performance appraisal, so that I could feel worthy to face another year as a valued member of the organization. My daughter's statement showed me, in many ways, I was renting out my self-esteem to other people, my worth and value were based on their interpretation of me. My children are not as much that way.

I am learning to free myself from the appraisal of other people and this has allowed me to stand alone over the past few years. My children taught me that—they are less needy than I am. My children often get upset about injustice, but I see this as a strength—they are sure about where they stand and do not need me or others to validate them. In this way their generation is free to pursue ideas, a mission and/or a purpose bigger than they are. I think we all want to be brave—something I see in my children every day—but sometimes bravery is the courage to stand alone.

> **As I have freed myself from the appraisal of others, this has freed me from needing to judge others and allowed me to be more uncertain, to see things from other points of view.**

As I have freed myself from the appraisal of others, this has freed me from needing to judge others and allowed me to be more uncertain, to see things from other points of view. When this happens, I find I am more compassionate, more tolerant, and care deeply about other people. I learned this from my children too. As they began to mature, I realized that they cared a lot about things that matter, and in many cases, they cared a lot more than I did. Imagine how humbling it must have been to see my children as more caring, compassionate, and kinder to others than I was!

My children care deeply about people—especially people in lower circumstances. Did you see on the news this past election who it was fighting for the minimum wage worker or the immigrant or the marginalized? Yup, those "terrible" millennials. Even though I claimed to follow God (I was a pastor for crying out loud!), I do not set a very good example for my children in this area. I grew up with the ideal of being "self-made." If something was wrong in life, pull up the boot straps and fix it! I think my generation has often felt the need to protect our tribe, to "Build the Wall," all while failing to realize the world is a community which needs to be nurtured.

My children seem to have a higher tolerance for uncertainty and mystery. I cannot understand how they can listen to podcasts over an hour long (I would never have enough patience for this). I listened to one of my daughters' podcasts the other day—several people with different opinions were featured and by the end they did not resolve a single thing. This was no NPR. I could not believe it, yet she said it was her favorite one!

My daughter and I were having a conversation awhile back and I do not remember what we were talking about, only that we never got to a resolution because she simply stated, "I have no idea." *How can you have no idea!?!?* To me, that is frightening! Whether I admitted it to her or not at the time is irrelevant now, but I have a deep need for certainty. I want to know what's wrong, who is responsible and how to fix it. I need my life to be broken down into 22-minute segments, a repeatable pattern of problem/solution. I need certainty.

My generation has made a lot of mistakes with certainty. Try discussing anything political with someone my own age, it is a nightmare! I used to be that way: "I am right—you are wrong—shut up and sit down (or go somewhere else if you do not like it)." Even the Bible has some uncertainty and mystery that requires trust and faith, something my generation and I are uncomfortable with. My children, the next generation, have taught me to become more comfortable and curious about mystery and less certain about the things I think I understand!

**If I am to be authentic, I can only say what I understand to be true and hope we can journey together toward the truth. Living authentically in this way requires more whimsy, I need to put it into practice.**

I am less judgmental these days, something I think my children have taught me. I used to have to prove I was always right when I talked about matters of faith with people. Now, I can discuss what I believe without telling them what they should believe. In this way I am discovering that in matters of faith there are mountains of things I do not fully understand. If I am to be authentic, I can only say what I understand to be true and hope we can journey together toward the truth. My children are proving it can be done in the way they engage with their neighbors, other cultures, and other faiths. I am glad they are less like me and that I am becoming more like them in this way.

I am grateful my children are concerned with the earth and its environment. I do not know who they learned that from as my generation has a long punch list of atrocities we have made environmentally. For many reasons even I ignored the signs, I assumed that it was either silly or unfruitful and have largely ignored environmental causes. My children have a sense of environmentalism because the health of the people, the planet, and the animals in it is deeply in jeopardy (just look at the number of species that have been moved from endangered to extinct from 2000 to 2010—it is shocking!) I am learning from my children that this is not about activism as much as personal responsibility. Veganism, environmentalism, and responsible agriculture will most likely be trends of the future.

I will be the first to admit I am not an expert on much of anything. But I do study things carefully. I have spent a long time studying the millennials, I raised three of them to adulthood, and I do not think I am wrong about them (there I go being certain again!). I have always been optimistic, but I do not think this is a superficial hope. I truly believe we are on the cusp of a major shift in religion, politics, and world affairs. I give much of the credit to Millennials for inspiring the changes. I think these can be positive changes. I hope I am right.

---

## FOR FURTHER THOUGHT

Reflect on the statements below. Don't overthink it, just let it flow. You can analyze it later.

1. What do you generally assume about people that are "other" than you?

2. What are some positive steps you can take concerning millennials?

3. What are several words that summarize your thoughts about this chapter or what is a quote you would like to remember?

# TRIBALISM, NATIONALISM, AND EMPIRE

One of my son's childhood friends hated Canada. I cannot remember him ever stating valid reasons for this ideology. I did not join him in his disdain for our Northern neighbor. It was almost a joke for my son and I to talk about this child's distaste for the Canucks. My son's friend generally mixed humor with whatever was troubling in his life, not liking the Canadians was some sort of coping mechanism to the pain in his life and possibly to the racism and tribalism that was all around him.

Small town America fosters an interesting form of tribalism. I was generally pleasant and neighborly except I could sometimes find myself in real battles over things like high school sports. I find it easy to become entrenched in religious and denominational exclusiveness. As a pastor in a small town, I saw some of the ugliest behavior between people living eight miles from each other. They can look the same, talk the same, eat the same foods, go to churches that sing the exact same songs, yet an athletic event held potential to turn into a border war that could go on for decades.

A new level of tribalism happens at the college level. All three of my children attended college. With the preparation that goes into sending a child to college, you would think that the final decision was well calculated. However, the decision was very limited by where we lived, how much money we had, the information we received, and our circumstances. I was surprised by my children's friends who picked a specific school because of something another friend told them—a "friend" who would likely abandon them soon after freshman orientation. That is just the way college works.

State and institutional level tribalism affects all of us. Laura graduated from the University of Texas and I lived near enough to the University of Oklahoma that I once rode my bicycle to the stadium. You would think our opinions of which institution and especially which football team is best would be based on something more scientific or rational than circumstances in our life that led us to pledge loyalty. Under pressure, I can espouse some excellent qualities of my school, but I did not even graduate from there. I got my first degree from a technical branch of the other large state school nearby. Loyalties were often based on circumstantial journeys that I had little control over, regardless, my loyalties ran deep.

Just yesterday, I was counting the number of Nebraskans that passed me on the interstate. With very little prompting, I can launch into sarcasms about how they are in a hurry to get out of their home state. Of course, driving itself creates tribalism. Everyone who drives slower than me is a "moron" and those that drive faster than me are surely "idiots." I seem to be in a hurry to generalize about people to try to make some sense out of my world, but I think there is something else going on here. Brené Brown calls this *Common Enemy Intimacy*:

> "Common Enemy Intimacy is counterfeit connection and the opposite of true belonging. If the bond we share with others is simply that we hate the same people, the intimacy we experience is often intense, immediately gratifying, and

an easy way to discharge outrage and pain. It is not, however, fuel for real connection."[1]

Being able to talk about the common things we do not like makes it easier to connect with people. I am often opinionated about my beliefs and it helps to have something in common that I do not like about others—talking about them helps form the new "us." Although it is a horrible basis for a friendship, it is one of the common strategies I find myself using to gain alliances. When I really want to get more people on my side, the first thing I feel I need to do is to find something that we communally dislike and focus on that. The fear of not fitting in and not belonging is stronger than the common sense to not behave in this manner, yet I find myself doing it all the time.

### Nationalism plays on my need to label and compare so that I feel superior to other peoples and promotes an "us versus them" mentality.

The natural next step is nationalism. Patriotism is probably not a bad thing in certain contexts; it is admirable when I love my country and when I am thankful for the sacrifices made by my ancestors. Patriotism can be a natural and beautiful thing, but it seems like patriotism often leads to nationalism. Nationalism plays on my need to label and compare so I can feel superior to other peoples and promotes an "us versus them" mentality. If we (my people) are not the best, it is probably their (the other team, side, nationality, etc.) fault. In nationalism, I begin to see other people as evil and as sub-human in one way or another. This nationalistic view is not congruent with the ways or the teaching of Jesus. Jesus went out of his way to teach and demonstrate this, especially with Samaritans. The early Christians taught that we are all a part of the same holy nation—there is no tribe or nation that is superior to another.[2]

To help us further discern the pitfalls of nationalism, I submit the example of Rome. At the time of Jesus, Rome was at the apex of its' nationalistic quest for empire. They had quite literally conquered the world. In terms of might, power, and luxury, they were the best! In areas that matter most like morality, spirituality, and welfare of mankind, they failed. Rome eventually would crumble–an inevitable fall to match its' meteoric rise. Countries like the United States seem to be headed in a similar direction—militarily and economically powerful, but morally bankrupt. If we continue our nationalistic pursuits, we will eventually fall prey to our passions. We do not have a magic elixir that precludes us from the inevitable.

Jesus began a very counter-cultural revolution in the first century. For the first 300 years, the church refused to join with the empire. It is one of the most amazing things ever witnessed in human history: a people, without a country or national identity, persecuted only to grow stronger. Occasionally in history, we see these same ideas resurrected in things like the Civil Rights movement and the times we battled for abolition of slavery and women's rights in the United States. We saw heroes like Nelson Mandela and Rosa Parks and Martin Luther King Jr. and Ruth Bader Ginsberg who suffered persecution to help free the oppressed. These people fought for equality, not superiority. They were continuing the revolution that Jesus started.

**According to Jesus' life and work, the second half of human history was supposed to be characterized by love, mercy, and grace.**

We should at least consider that if Jesus physically were present today, he would not pledge allegiance to any nation. How could he build walls between his American and Mexican children? He would not join a local church or pledge allegiance to any denomination. He would not be Protestant or Catholic or Buddhist or Muslim. He would never rally for violence, retribution, or competition between nations.

It is currently Advent season as I write. Yesterday I listened to a sermon by Brian Zahnd about how human history began in a cave with paintings of animals on the wall and the second half of human history was inaugurated by Jesus being born in a cave with live animals nearby. According to Jesus' life and work, the second half of human history was supposed to be characterized by love, mercy, and grace. The failed experiment of nationalism and empire had been teased out by the Romans to its inevitable conclusion. It failed and should never be tried again. We should avoid returning to failed experiments of the past, like nationalism, at all costs.

My son and his friend turned out to be fine people. From the trials of their youth, they emerged as beautiful human beings who embody love and compassion for all peoples. They are both strong sports fans and seem to have a reasonable perspective on that level of tribalism—it is all fun and not real life. My son has taught me a deeper type of compassion, because of him I have learned a deeper empathy for all people. He lives oversees and genuinely has a great confidence in himself without ever having to hate anyone. My daughters are the same—they seem to have developed a compassion for those others want to hate. I admire them all and by the grace of God, I think they are leading me home!

Not long ago, I realized I was making all kinds of excuses for the way I was behaving. I determined that perhaps it was time for me to stop making excuses. I can strive for excellence personally without dehumanizing those who are inconvenient to love. I am learning to love my friends and make new friends by loving my "enemies." I am striving to ground my self-worth in my ability to create and build instead of my capacity to destroy and tear down. I can embrace the refugee without fear because I first embraced RefuJesus. I can love the whole world if I begin to speak like the poets and the prophets and imagine something better.

---

## FOR FURTHER THOUGHT

Reflect on the statements below. Don't overthink it, just let it flow. You can analyze it later.

1. Describe some local tribalism where you live.

2. Brainstorm about some ways that nationalism, tribalism, and loyalty to empire can be detrimental to us. What would you like to change about your practices?

3. Imagine that Jesus came to visit your home for a couple of weeks. Try to process what you would do and where you would take him. Would he go to political rally? Which side would he be on or would he even take a side? Where would you go to church or would you even go to church or possibly take him to a synagogue? Who would he want to talk to? What would he do during the Star Spangled Banner (take a knee or stand at attention)? Would he agree that the United States is a Christian nation?

4. What are several words that summarize your thoughts about this chapter or what is a quote you would like to remember?

# VIOLENCE AND WAR

I remember when Laura and I tried to help my son discover what he wanted to do with the rest of his life. I wanted my children to be able to do what they wanted so I did not try to push them into a particular field. I knew that getting a collegiate degree would give them some advantages, and like most parents, I worried about paying for it. Naturally, I wanted my children to consider entering military service as an option (because it would pay for college). My grandfather served in World War 2 and my uncle served in Vietnam. My brother-in-law and my brother were both in the military. For this and other reasons, I admire and respect those who risk their lives in military service. War seemed like an inevitable reality of the world I was in. I thought it seemed logical to consider military service to avoid the cost of sending a child through college and, as a side benefit, it would teach them some discipline.

Laura had a different opinion.

The military represented sending her only son into the ravages of war and facing the possibility he may never come home. For some unknown reason, my son was not the least bit interested in military service. He was not concerned with the financial challenges of college; he had more faith in my provision than I had. I had to put aside the image of my son dressed in his military whites coming home with medals hanging off his chest and I set about trying to finance a college education in the most reasonable way possible. My son would have to work but at least he would not have to risk his life, and for the moment, that made everyone happy.

**Although I knew Jesus' teaching on violence, I set that aside for the moment and enjoyed the pride of being American.**

When the World Trade Center was bombed on September 11, 2001, like most Americans, I was tuned in. *How could this happen?* I felt as if the world was coming to an end. Watching the towers fall on the television was like watching an action movie with people scurrying into buildings as the huge cloud of dust rolled down the narrow streets. Then, a few days later, George W. Bush stood on the rubble and vowed revenge for the atrocities that happened on 9/11 and I felt some hope. Like most Americans, I watched from the comfort of my living room as the U.S. invaded Afghanistan and Iraq over the next few months. I felt vindicated, someone had stood up for me and it provided some sort of justice. Although I knew Jesus' teaching on violence, I set it aside for the moment and enjoyed the pride of being American.

On a visit to Washington D.C. years later, Laura and I went on a night tour. We saw lighted buildings like the Jefferson and Lincoln monuments and most of the war memorials. It was stunning and beautiful, and our tour guide really made it fun. The most striking of the monuments was by far the Korean War memorial. If you have never seen it, the soldiers all wear raincoats and seem to be rising out of the marsh. At least that is the way I remember it. The memorial was dimly lit and left me with a kind of sadness I could not quite explain. My mind immediately went to my grandpa who was involved in the second World War. As far as I know he was never injured, but I remember asking him about the war he never talked about. He donated his medals and uniforms to charity and refused to discuss what he experienced there. I thought of my uncle who was injured in Vietnam and suffered tremendously until he passed away somewhat prematurely. I cried softly to myself—I was not angry—just sad.

I cannot speak for all people, but most of the time I did what I had to do to survive. When I consider painful or troubling things, I often make certain justifications in my mind or refuse to dwell on them. When I consider all the horrible things in the world, I often build my philosophies and theologies around what I think I need to do to survive.

The early church faced intense persecution for the first 300 years, it flourished in many ways, but suffered none-the-less. Eventually Constantine was able to convince the church to join forces with the Empire—the same Empire that was killing them—and, in a relatively short amount of time, Christians were killing other Christians. Religion became organized and stable, but also repressed Jesus' teaching about non-violence to advocate the current practices and policies on "just" wars and "just" killings. They still said, "love your neighbor," but like the disciples[1], re-drew some of the boundaries of who was their neighbor and who was their enemy.

Since the 4th century, God's people have been involved in almost every kind of war imaginable. Hitler's army was comprised mostly of Catholic and Protestant Christians. We have somehow justified the killing of millions of other people, mostly because they were not "us" or they were against us. Genocide of Native Americans, slavery, apartheid, world wars, military actions, civil wars, gang wars, school shootings—the list seems endless!

*While his Jewish culture was hoping he would bring justice in the form of military might, he stayed true to his message of non-violence, love of enemies, and compassion for all peoples.*

Something changed in my worldview a few years ago. Up until then, I had accepted that violence was simply a reality of life and I assumed even God understood we could only take so much. After all, he is portrayed as angry and retributive at times. But Jesus did not accept that supposed reality. When the Empire that encircled his world promoted a culture of violence and conquest, Jesus offered an alternative reality of peace. While his Jewish culture was hoping he would bring justice in the form of military might, he stayed true to his message of non-violence, love of enemies, and compassion for all peoples. Slowly, I began to accept the Jesus paradigm with all its mystery, uncertainty, and paradox.

I do not have an end to this story. I live in a country that has made nationalism into an alternative religion. The "us against them" sentiment is strong, even among those that follow the Prince of Peace. I do not know how this story is going to end. It seems that one option is to keep killing each other and hope like hell that God is on our side. I find that hard to fathom now especially since my country has spent most of its short history exterminating the natives of its' land, enslaving people from another continent, and engaging in wars at every opportunity.

With all the blood on our hands, the possibility or probability of God being on our side (if that is even a thing) seems unlikely.

The other outcome, although improbable, is to follow the prophets and poets and imagine an alternative outcome. If we choose to, we can imagine and work toward a world that Jesus believed was possible. It is a world that loves its' enemy and does not return evil for evil but pays back evil with good. We can begin with our own small worlds (tribes) and change them first to a place that sees love, peace, grace, and mercy as priorities and not as exceptions. We can encourage and promote companies to put people over profit. Organizations exists first for the common good and not just to "win."

## *We do not have to trash the whole experiment, but let's take a hard look at our religion and our society, please!*

Just like Jesus, when I begin to speak this way, people begin to accuse me of not loving my country or being against the military or some other nonsense. Nothing could be further from the truth! I am extremely impressed with this amazing experiment called the United States and also of the American church. But, just like with any experiment, we need to examine the parts of the experiment that have failed. How about we imagine (hypothesize) a new way of tackling the problems we face? We do not have to trash the whole experiment, but let's take a hard look at our religion and our society, please! Those of us who claim to be followers of Jesus need to put his ideas into practice.

Maybe we should make the second 250 years of our country be less like Constantine and more like Jesus. Is it possible to become comfortable with mystery and paradox and less dualistic? Imagine not having to "win" by putting more focus on what we become.

Some days I find it hard to be optimistic and easier to accept things as they are. But Americans and Christians have always been dreamers. I hope more and more we can begin to realize the dream of living in the society that Jesus imagined: a world of love, a world of peace, and a world of genuine hope.

My son eventually did go overseas after he graduated from college. He currently lives in Taiwan where he teaches English. Taiwan is a very peaceful country and safe to abide in. This makes Laura happy. I was struck by the friendliness of everyone I met there on my last visit. Ironically, I seemed to experience that dream Jesus had of an alternative society more in Taiwan than I do in my home country that imagines itself as a Christian nation. Before anyone lights the torches and says, "Move there if I love it so much," please do not misunderstand. All I am saying is that Jesus' dream is possible. It is possible to love our neighbor, to treat people with respect, to worry less about being the best and more about being what we should.

Taiwan and my son have inspired in me a hope that Jesus' dream of a better world is still alive—it is still possible—and it is still the best option. It's not that my son or Taiwan are perfect, it's just that I get encouraged when I see people striving for progress. I witnessed it again recently here at home when local people raised money for my grandson's surgery. It gives me hope for the future. I hope we can hang on to that non-violent hope that Jesus set before us. It is the Father's heart for his children.

## FOR FURTHER THOUGHT

Reflect on the statements below. Don't overthink it, just let it flow. You can analyze it later.

1. Consider your thoughts about violence and wars.

   - Are they necessary?

   - What is your assessment of the first 300 years of the church?

   - Is self-defense okay?

   - How do you reconcile the violence of the Old Testament with the Sermon on the Mount and Jesus' other teaching?

2. What are several words that summarize your thoughts about this chapter or what is a quote you would like to remember?

# REJECTED BY GOD?

I have had thick glasses since I was about five; when you have glasses like mine, it is easy to get classified as smart and/or a little crazy. Growing up I was relatively short. I am not sure why most societies honor the taller people, but I seemed to never get picked for the team—no matter what game we were playing. The fact that my family growing up was relatively poor did not help either. Short, skinny, relatively low economic status, and glasses—from the pictures, I gather this led to some poor wardrobe choices. All this left me with an intense desire to fit in.

To make it worse, when I was seven years old a preacher convinced me I was rejected by God. Even now, I am trying to take inventory of just how evil a young man can be as a seven-year-old. I know it was not adultery and I hadn't murdered anyone; I was not to the lusting stage yet and I hadn't yet learned how to steal (that would come later when I went to a Christian school); I did not carve out any graven images and I had not yet learned how to cuss (again, the Christian school would help me learn that skill). There is always the possibility of not honoring my father and mother—but, for a timid soul, I am not sure that was a big issue. I kept the sabbath holy because I did not have a choice. I am pretty sure, at seven-years-old, it boiled down to coveting. From the time I was old enough to speak I wanted other children's toys and vehemently yelled, "Mine!" So…God was going to torture me for that? The preacher did not use the word rejected. I was told that God had *turned his back* on me; kind of seems like the same thing to me.

No need to worry though—I walked to the front of the church that day, said the sinner's prayer, and later the same month I got baptized. However, that did not stop me from sinning. In fact, later in life, I learned bigger and worse sins. I learned how to steal and lust, along with a myriad of other things prohibited by denomination and the Bible. I would have been classified as mischievous by most; the system I was in promoted shaming those that stepped outside of the boundaries of good behavior. These layers of shame and rejection built up inside me and I continued to shove them down. Eventually the trash bag overflowed, and I was left with the nagging feeling I did not belong. I was so sure God would never accept me. How could he with all the filth I had held inside?

When I had children, my experience of love and rejection got mixed up. I experienced love and affection like I had never felt, but also, I felt rejection like I would never have imagined. Most of the rejection I felt was simply my children transitioning through different stages in life and I was not prepared for those transformations. I felt it when my children preferred to play with their friends instead of me or when they chose to stay out all night with friends "just to talk." When they were teenagers, they would lock themselves in their room and only come out for feedings and to find lost clothing items. "Go to your room" used to be a form of punishment but now it was punishing me.

I experienced feelings of rejection when they went to college. I felt rejected when they dated. At almost every stage of their lives, Laura had to explain to me that they were changing and doing what was natural. I felt rejection, but they were not rejecting me, they were going through a natural separation necessary to become responsible, independent adults. My children were quickly outgrowing, outpacing me. I was not chosen to be on their team—I was the short, wardrobe malfunctioned, seven-year-old boy with thick glasses all over again.

Remember the story about the preacher from earlier? I heard his voice in those moments with my children. I felt God was disappointed in my behavior as a parent. I did not shake my fist at God or wreck his car or destroy his favorite memorabilia, I was the same seven-year-old confused little child that believed everyone had rejected him.

At this point, I briefly thought it would be natural to take my feelings of rejection and just go ahead and reject my children. After all, if that is what God does, it must be okay. These feelings were very strong during their high school and early college years. My initial thoughts were probably something like "They do not want me—I do not want them." Maybe I should just "turn my back on them" and get on with my life. I have seen some parents say to their children, "You are no longer my son/daughter." But I could not do it! I cannot imagine doing so as a parent and I certainly cannot imagine God stooping to that level. If I was not able to do it, then how could God turn his back on me?

The story of how the Father feels about us is illustrated in the Parable of the Prodigal Son that shows the Father's heart even after the son has rejected him and run away to spend his inheritance. When the son returns, the father races to meet him. The father let the child leave, but when the child was ready, the father rushed to meet him. When the child was at his worst, the father was watching and waiting for him. When the son changed his mind, the father revealed that his mind remained the same—he loved him. I have not always been like that, but I am learning.

What I want to believe is this: when we are at our worst, like a good parent, God draws closer to us, not further away. When I feel rejection, it is because of my own faulty understanding. To reject someone is to exhibit childish and adolescent behavior. Rejection is not a quality I can honestly ascribe to a God who is supposed to be love. I am not a great parent, but God is at least better than me. Rejection is not helpful—it is hurtful. It has taken at least half of my life to get over the repercussions of rejection. I cannot accept that God rejects us. I can only accept that as a good parent and a God of love he would notice my behavior, draw close to me, and say very simply, "I am with you."

---

## FOR FURTHER THOUGHT

Reflect on the statements below. Don't overthink it, just let it flow. You can analyze it later.

1. Think about past rejections in your life.

2. How do you currently feel about the idea that God would reject you?

   • Does it make you mad?

   • Does it worry you?

3. Think about what it would be like to be totally accepted. Think about a time when you felt accepted and consider what it would be like to feel that way consistently?

4. On a scale of one to ten consider how accepted you feel and why that is.

5. What are several words that summarize your thoughts about this chapter or what is a quote you would like to remember?

# NONE OF US IS RIGHT

I tend to get distracted. I am not very focused when it comes to digesting lectures. I like to read books for this very reason—I can go back and re-read when my mind wanders. Every so often in a lecture, I hear something that makes me want to stop the speaker and say, "Back the truck up. Could you repeat that? Did I hear you right?" I was quite impressed with the speaker during a recent lecture I attended. I cannot say that Sister Judith Sutera had my total attention, however.

Like any good speaker, Sister Judith did not fully exhaust the topic of the day and left some mystery behind it. On the board she wrote, "None of us is right!", turned, and just looked at us. She seemed to realize that some of us had just had our minds blown and would need a moment to wipe brain matter off the clothing of the person next to us. With precision and accuracy, I had heard that one statement and it stuck. *None of us is right!?!?!*

Her statement was shocking, being especially appropriate to my journey at the time. I am sure I sat up a little straighter and, at least for a few minutes, gave her my full attention.

For a good portion of my life, I was associated with religious people that banked everything on being certain. They possessed a series of beliefs that they knew were right and did not allow any room to question or debate those beliefs and assumptions. Being right was something they were sure of and to be anything less could bring scorn, ridicule, and potentially some form of exclusion. Whether these certainties were affirmed 100 years ago or 500 really did not matter, there was a line in the sand, and it was not to be crossed.

> **At some point there comes a time when you raise your hand to God (in one way or another) and say, "I agree to promote and defend these particular beliefs."**

As a pastor, I was counseled to make sure I knew how I felt about certain issues. I was encouraged to know what I believed but also encouraged to stay within the framework that was provided—after all, it was Biblical. Notwithstanding the hundreds of other denominational belief systems that also claimed to be right, many of them also Biblical. At some point there comes a time when you raise your hand to God (in one way or another) and say, "I agree to promote and defend these particular beliefs." Most church members go through something similar. For pastors, we call it ordination. For members, we might call it membership, or possibly "indoctrination." There is nothing wrong with being formed and forming beliefs. But, when I am too certain and reject the mystery of faith in a God who spat into a man's eyes to heal him, raised the dead to life, and turned water into the best wine found anywhere on the planet, certainty can and does lead to problems.

Like I said, I came to a point in my life where I started to question my certainties. *Maybe I am wrong.* When I opened to this possibility, I found all kinds of beauty in my life and understanding of God. I found God to be restorative, instead of retributive. I found God to be more Christ-like, faith to be loving and full of grace. I found communities that are open and accepting of all peoples instead of exclusive. I watched my children grow up and question their foundational beliefs to develop their own beautiful methodologies. This new approach to life, love, and family made sense to me. I saw others as Christ would, fulfilling his injunction to love. In short, my children influenced me—something I always hoped would happen.

Sister Judith stood there looking at us with, *"None of us is right,"* written on the chalkboard just above her shoulder. At first glance, this might sound discouraging but it was not. To know none of us are right keeps me on the journey, to know none of us has it all figured out keeps me humble. I can be more accepting of those who disagree with me because I know I am not perfect either. I love that my children have less of a problem saying, "I do not know," and, "I do not have all the answers." It is very liberating to be able to acknowledge other beliefs even if they are not exactly like mine.

I know that none of us is right. I now understand that it is the journey that affects my understanding. Now that may sound scary, but to me it is comforting. I know God can bring me to the right understanding because he is constantly walking with me in this mysterious journey of understanding. By starting from the understanding that I am *not* right, I continue the journey of learning and growing, and I will be able to live with the paradox and mystery that comes with it.

I thank my children for inviting me on this journey and walking it with me.

## FOR FURTHER THOUGHT

Reflect on the statements below. Don't overthink it, just let it flow. You can analyze it later.

1. Consider the statement "none of us is right."

   • What implications does it have?

   • What emotions does the statement "none of us is right" stir up in you?

   • Imagine what positive benefits could come from affirming this statement.

2. Consider what pledging allegiance to a belief system may have cost you in the past.

3. What are several words that summarize your thoughts about this chapter or what is a quote you would like to remember?

# THE PERILS OF FEAR

When my children were young, I encouraged them to be brave. When a tooth needed to be pulled or they needed to learn to answer the phone, I would quietly whisper in their ear, *"Be brave"*. I wanted my children to learn bravery because I saw people all around me whose lives were ruled by fear and I did not want that type of life for my children. I knew I had succeeded as a parent when one day I heard my older daughter tell my younger daughter to *"be brave"* when she was facing her own crisis of confidence. In this way, all my children are now self-sufficient, confident, and conquerors of their own little worlds in their own little ways.

Several years ago, I began to realize that while I was encouraging my children to be brave and not be afraid, I was in many ways peddling fear as an evangelical preacher. I noticed that before I could sell "salvation" I had to scare them just enough so they would want what I was offering. I never did this consciously; it was just a way of doing business. I liked to hear preachers "step on my toes," because it felt good when they solved my problems a half hour later. By default, I was doing the same thing with my children. This is what I was taught and what I felt comfortable with.

In addition to the practice of preaching, I was inclined to fear the unknown. I was part of a system of rules designed to alleviate those concerns. Even though Jesus and the New Testament seemed to say in various ways "do not fear," most modern religious systems seemed to thrive on at least a nominal amount of fear. Bertrand Russell, an atheist, stated in his 1927 lecture *Why I am not a Christian*:

> "Religion is based primarily and mainly upon fear. It is partly the terror of the unknown and partly the wish to feel that you have a kind of elder brother who will stand by you in all your troubles and disputes. My Fear is the basis of the whole thing – fear of the mysterious, fear of defeat, fear of death."[1]

My religious systems countered fear with various strategies of control. At times I even stated, "God is in control." I needed to believe that God was in control so that I would not be afraid. While that was true in the sense of things like gravity and natural laws and the fact that I take breaths without conscious effort, God does not physically or mentally control my actions. He cannot force me or scare me or even guilt me into doing his will. He draws me and invites me to do what is right, I thought I needed control to not be afraid.

Fear not only affected my religious life, it bled into my personal life as well. I found myself doing just enough to be successful, then relax into a routine that felt safe. Often my greatest dreams were unrealized because I was afraid to risk what was necessary to achieve them. Recently, I heard an actor state, *"Your wildest dreams are on the other side of your fear."*[2] Everything that is worth doing involves some vulnerability, some moderate risk and a fair amount of courage.

The believers in the New Testament church faced unbelievable challenges every day. The book of Hebrews describes approximately 12-15 ways the new believers suffered in just four verses (Hebrews 11:35-38). One of those ways was "being sawed in two." Yikes! From "jeers" to death, it was a certainty that the new church would suffer. But, the consistent message of God for the church was always, "do not fear" and "don't be afraid."

John tells us that love and fear are incompatible and love is supposed to be the main purpose of everything (1 John 4:18-19). Occasionally, I noticed my fear caused me to be angry or cruel to others. When fear is present, you can either run away or freeze up or come out swinging. Even if we've never thrown a punch, most of us know how to intimidate, criticize, or humiliate those who would dare to make us feel threatened. I found myself responding to situations in my life instead of loving people in the way Jesus taught.

Over time, due in part to the example of my children, I began to wonder, "What if my guiding motivation was love? If perfect love casts out fear, could I love more by recognizing God as bigger than my fear?" I began to hope that my voice and my life would be less of a response to the world, even less of a response to other Christians, and more of a witness to them instead.

I cannot say that my children are fearless, but they are courageous. Love takes courage, which is why love casts out fear. My children reinforced that lesson with me. I have seen them try to love the less fortunate, love the helpless and the marginalized, love those who live on the fringes of society even when no one else sees them doing it. I am learning from my children to love people in courageous ways. I find this brand of love exciting, but it often scares me to death. So, when I find myself wanting to be afraid, when I want to run away, when I want to hide, I look up in trust. And I hear the Father of all whisper into my ear, "Be brave my son, be brave."

## FOR FURTHER THOUGHT

Reflect on the statements below. Don't overthink it, just let it flow. You can analyze it later.

1. Make a mental list of everything you are afraid of (real or imagined).

2. What is it costing you to carry that fear with you?

3. What are some positive steps you could take this week to step into that fear?

4. What are the obstacles to stepping into the fear and being vulnerable?

5. What are several words that summarize your thoughts about this chapter or what is a quote you would like to remember?

# JUSTICE

"The arc of the moral universe is long, but it bends toward justice."

**—MARTIN LUTHER KING JR.**

"God blesses those who hunger and thirst for justice..."

**—JESUS**

One of my daughters always wanted things to be fair when she was growing up. She was not petty or mean about it and it was not like she counted her Christmas gifts, she just occasionally reminded me about the ways that I was more generous to one child or the other. Laura has similar tendencies, she wants everyone to have the same number of gifts in their stockings and makes sure that if one child gets a gift, the other child must have an equivalent number of gifts at the same approximate cost.

I did not expect life to be fair. I assumed it was not and I was determined to work hard enough to overcome whatever injustices there were in life. A part of me wants to help others overcome things that are not fair, and another part wants someone or something else to step in and make things right. I guess I sympathize with both views. Why can't a more powerful being than I bring about rightness or fairness or justice to my world? I often hope to find this quality in leaders, and it is what I hope to find in God. I hear people say, *"God is love, but he is also justice."* I am learning about how *"God is love"*, but what do we mean when we call God just?

I used to think the term justice referred to the idea that things will be better if people were punished for what they did wrong. This created an imbalance to God's justice, because I want God to forgive me, but I want him to punish others for what they do wrong in my eyes. In this way, God's justice is retributive. Ever since Cain killed Abel, there has been a deep-seated longing for justice in the form of retribution. Either the offender gets paid back in some sort of revenge plot or pays their debt to society by being "locked up" for some arbitrary length of time.

My children view God differently though and I am learning from them to believe in fairness. Like many in recent times, my children have concluded that retributive justice usually doesn't reform people, and, if the victims do not find some peace internally, none of this really makes anyone feel better long term. I have always had the suspicion that this really was not what God had in mind. Recently, my views have been changing toward a different brand of justice that I see reflected in Jesus' words and actions. To get some perspective, I asked a Facebook community to give me their definition of justice. Here are some of the responses I received.

Justice is:

- "…the state or condition in which everything and everyone in the created order is in right relationship with each other and can reach their God-given potential."

- "…setting things right."

- "...everything sad becoming untrue (Tolkien)."

- "...communal, a state of well-being in which all wrongs have been righted and all members are regarded and treated equally."

- "...the restoration of wholeness, or a move toward wholeness."

- "...the broken are healed."

- "...reordering, renewal, and restoration of all things."

- "...God's love expressed."

- "...all power expressed only in the service of others, especially the weakest."

- "...the correct balance of social equality that is reflective of God's goodness."

As you may have gathered, this type of *restorative* justice reflects Jesus. Restorative justice is when God makes things right and is based primarily in his love. I think the solution is found somewhere in the definitions above as well as in the life and teachings of Jesus.

It is Christmas day again and I was inclined not to write today but here I am. What could be more appropriate to write about on Christmas day than God's justice? Jesus came to bring justice to the world, to set things right for the sinner. His way was forgiveness, mercy, love, and peace. These are the things that restore, they are the things that Jesus taught. To love our enemies, do good to those that hurt us, and turn the other cheek, this is what brings restoration. This is justice!

Today, I held my grandson, Jackson (whom I call J.B.). J.B. was born eight weeks premature and I did not get to hold him until recently. As he looked into my eyes, I was filled with desire for justice. I want to leave my children and grandchildren a world where they can prosper, be challenged, and live in peace. I want them to experience love, grace, mercy–and I want them to find justice. Not the kind that seeks to fix the world through punishment. I want them to find the justice of the God of Christmas Day, a God who sets things right in the world, a God who restores in love.

Merry Christmas!

---

## FOR FURTHER THOUGHT

Reflect on the statements below. Don't overthink it, just let it flow. You can analyze it later.

1. If a simple definition of justice is "setting things right," consider a world where things are set right.

   - What would this new world look like?

   - What do you think Jesus was talking about when he mentioned justice?

   - How do people sometimes misinterpret the idea of justice?

2. What are several words that summarize your thoughts about this chapter or what is a quote you would like to remember?

# PURPOSE

None of our children considered going into, "ministry." I was a professional pastor for 20 years and they likely saw firsthand how ministry can be painful at times. My children seemed to have gleaned the good from church life (like love your neighbor, to have mercy and compassion), and they threw away the bad. I am not surprised they did not want to follow in my footsteps. There are many pitfalls and challenges to ministry, and I do not even know if I want them to follow my previous professional path. Being a pastor was rewarding, but over time I felt that the role I played in church was not the way it was originally intended.

Right now, I am considering what I will do with the next phase of my life. I find that I am no longer comfortable labeling things as, "God's Work," or describing my purpose as being "used by God." I no longer see ministry jobs as more important than other vocations and most of the evangelical jargon does not work for me anymore. So, when I need to focus, I try to go back to basics. I defer to the prophet Micah:

> "He has showed you, O man, what is good; and what does the Lord require of you but to do justice, and to love kindness, and to walk humbly with your God?"

Justice, kindness (mercy), and humility are recurring themes in Scripture. The Hebrew word for Justice is *mishpat* and carries with it the idea of having our case heard. This is justice in the sense of making things right, not revenge or punishment. The focus is on restoring those who have fallen or made mistakes. In similar fashion, mercy is not giving people what they deserve. It is a primary characteristic of God and is sometimes translated kindness. It is kindness in every circumstance. Humility may be the most basic of all human virtues. Humility may be the most important of the three as I think seeing ourselves correctly is one of the most central and vital qualities we can possess.

I was in ministry off and on for 20 years. Initially, I was a lead pastor at a startup church in a small town. We built the church building and even though we had some challenges, we had positive impact on people. When the local school was in danger of closing, my family and I moved across the river where I pastored another church and had a second job at a plant that manufactured ethanol. This second church also had some successes as well as challenges. After 13 years of this, we took a break before agreeing to re-plant a church in a somewhat larger city nearby. At this time, I was entering a sort of deconstruction of my beliefs and after three years at the re-plant, I resigned to see if I could figure out who I was and where I was going.

I have worked in several professions and have a few degrees. Before becoming a pastor, I was a computer programmer. During my second two tenures as a pastor, I worked at the ethanol plant in various capacities. I was an operator, then a Quality Assurance Manager, and later a Safety Manager. I loved learning about my professions and picked up my second bachelor's degree while working at the ethanol plant.

In my many professions, I have seen a lot of things that discouraged and confused me. I saw religion that was based primarily on fear and control. I saw belief systems that seemed to picture God as Zeus or Santa Claus instead of Jesus. I found I had to attend to the business of doing church and did not notice the spirituality of the actual church was lacking. I saw the futility of chasing after career aspirations, but I also realized the frustrations of trying to be more Christ-like in a system that at times was broken.

At this very moment, I find myself in a reconstruction of my faith as well as another career change. During the second half of my life I want to get my beliefs right. This could be my need for certainty creeping back in or hopefully it is me trying to live my life in a way that is authentic and true. I do not think this is a mid-life crisis—it is an adjustment. I want to live my best life in the time I have remaining. What is best is to find ways that I can make things right for others—what is best is to not just to give people what they deserve—what is best is to be sure and certain, but not prideful.

In many ways, my children tend to fight for what is good as well - they love justice, mercy, and are humble beings. My children are not vengeful, and they do not live reactively, they do fight for justice and see the people who live on the fringes of society. Laura and I sometimes joke that we want to grow up to be like our children I am not at all discouraged that my children did not follow in my footsteps. I see now that they are choosing to follow Jesus instead of me. When I look down at my feet, I find I am following in their footsteps, instead of them following in mine. I am at peace with that.

My children have directly modeled what is good. Maybe trying to find our purpose is not as important as finding our character, not so much about what we do as to what we become.

## FOR FURTHER THOUGHT

Reflect on the statements below. Don't overthink it, just let it flow. You can analyze it later.

1. What does it mean to *do justice?*

2. What does it mean to *love kindness?*

3. What does it mean to *walk humbly?*

4. Take some time and try to describe what your purpose is.

5. What are several words that summarize your thoughts about this chapter or what is a quote you would like to remember?

# DARKNESS AND SHADOW

I grew up in a large family where it was never quiet. Nothing was ever totally still and there was never complete darkness. There always seemed to be a light on somewhere and, when I was young, I could fall asleep anywhere except in the dark. My children, too, could never sleep in total darkness. Fear of the dark seems to be a common human tendency. In most religions, light is seen as a positive thing. Believers are encouraged to walk in the light or be the light or simply be enlightened.

Carl Jung, the noted psychiatrist and psychoanalyst who founded analytical psychology, made the statement:

"One does not become enlightened by imagining figures of light, but by making the darkness conscious."

Jung, and other more recent figures, believe we all have something called a shadow. In his book, *Bringing the Shadows Out of the Dark,* Robert August Masters describes the shadow as *"our internal storehouse for anything in us we have disowned or rejected, or are otherwise keeping in the dark—things such as anger, shame, empathy, grief, vulnerability, and unresolved wounding."* For reasons of survival, we deny or bury our deeper pain and core wounding. The shadow contains what we do not know, do not like, or deny about ourselves. Masters further explains: *"The more we push it* [the shadow] *away or ignore it, the stronger and more rooted it becomes, insinuating its way into our everyday life."*

My friend, Dr. Paul Fitzgerald, recently helped me walk through addressing some shadow issues in my life. He and my spiritual director held my hand (figuratively) through this process. I consider addressing my shadow to be one of the best things that has ever happened to me.

In the past, I experienced a religious life where people used spiritual language to bypass issues related to the shadow. These psychological issues could be signs of trauma or wounding and often religious people would attempt to bypass these issues with a quick spiritual fix that excused the seriousness of the problem. Although good intentioned, often these quick fixes cause the shadow issues to become more pronounced, wounding us further. When the shadow is ignored it tends to come out in reactive, blaming, and irrational ways. This is why a normally stable board member blows up in a church council meeting or why a husband suddenly blames his wife for all the troubles in his life. However irrational it may seem, this type of behavior is not the conscious self but the unconscious heart of a much younger self that was wounded and buried that pain to survive. Even good things like empathy can be suppressed when it helps the survival of the individual.

In my case, the areas that I was disowning were things like rejection and fear. Instead of facing them, I kept them repressed until they came out in reactionary behavior.

Many times, our religious conditioning can cause things to remain packed away in our shadow until we investigate it. We are reactive because we operate on autopilot losing our core self or essential individuality. Problems with the shadow happen when it breaks out and misbehaves. Unless we bravely encounter and own our shadow, we will always be faced with the unpredictable return of what we suppress. While this all sounded a little mystical to me at the beginning, by the end I found it to be very true and very helpful.

My shadow work began when I read the following statement from Masters' book:

> "One of the first steps in healing this dynamic (shame) is to bring its origins out of the shadow and get in between our inner child and our inner critic, identifying with neither while loving and protecting the child in us. We then neither lose ourselves in our shame nor flee it. We are present to it, holding it with a well-grounded awareness."

My son, in his early years, would often swagger out of his room, gun in holster, cowboy boots on, ready for action. Except, he was only wearing his underwear. He would often walk around the house dressed this way, holding my hand, all his faith put in my ability to protect and provide for him. When I think of my own inner child, I see myself standing there coming out of my own inner room, wearing not underwear but my own insecurities and frailties, gun in holster, ready for action. However, often there was no one there to hold my hand and I received some bad feedback. Thus, my shadow self was formed when I pressed down those emotions.

When I think about my current struggles, I can see how my inner child and the inner critic have been responding from the shadow and ignoring my conscious mind. When this happens, I tell my younger self (Joey) very simply, *"I have your back."* I want him to know that he does not have to be afraid because I am holding his hand. I am stronger than his fears, insecurities, and frailties - I am able to assure him that I can keep him safe. This is a conscious look at my unconscious soul. When I did this the first time, I began to weep in a way that I do not believe I ever have. I cried out, "Oh God!", but I could not say anything else. I simply began to think about my children, their courage, and my hopes for them.

Afterward, I felt a peace like I have not felt in a long time—maybe never. I made a list of all the times I had been rejected and forgave those people. I released some current struggles I was having and simply sat in genuine light. Often though we avoid this healing due to spiritual bypassing.

Masters also talks about the tendency toward spiritual bypassing:

> "Spiritual bypassing is the use of spiritual practices and beliefs to avoid dealing with our painful feelings, unresolved wounds, and developmental needs. It is much more common than we might think and, in fact, is so pervasive as to go largely unnoticed, except in its more obvious extremes."

Aspects of spiritual bypassing include exaggerated detachment, emotional numbing and repression, overemphasis on the positive, anger-phobia, blind or overly tolerant compassion, weak or too porous boundaries, lopsided development (cognitive intelligence often being far ahead of emotional and moral intelligence), debilitating judgment about one's negativity or shadow elements, devaluation of the personal relative to the spiritual, and delusions of having arrived at a higher level of being.

Spiritual bypassing is common, but it doesn't solve our core problems. Healing core issues that plague us takes work and time. I can only offer you my testimony of how I am better because I stepped into the darkness and interacted with the shadow lurking there. As Jung stressed, we must become "conscious of the darkness," only then can we begin to unravel the unconscious hold it has on us.

Now that they are grown, my children no longer need a night light in order to sleep. I am finding that I can sleep in the dark too, I do not need a constant sense of motion, noise, or presence. I have encountered my shadow, stepped into the darkness wearing all my insecurities, gun in holster, ready for action. And in that place of shadow, I feel a strong hand holding mine, a soft whisper tickles my ear, "I've got your back." I feel much more safe—much more free.

---

## FOR FURTHER THOUGHT

Reflect on the statements below. Don't overthink it, just let it flow. You can analyze it later.

1. Take some time to meditate on the things you might have been surprised by.

2. Reflect on the times that you were reactionary, blaming, or unstable.

3. Consider that you have an inner child. What are some messages he/she is currently feeling or saying to you?

4. Consider that you also have an *inner critic*. What are some messages this critic keeps repeating to you?

5. Take time to sit with both of them. Stand up to the inner critic and stand with the inner child. Make sure to enlist a good counselor or spiritual director to walk with you.

6. What are several words that summarize your thoughts about this chapter or what is a quote you would like to remember?

# THE NEXT COURAGEOUS STEP

All the women in my house suddenly gathered around our grandson Jackson. We were celebrating Christmas a couple of days late and opening gifts. My mother-in-law, Shirley, was holding this child that was born eight weeks premature. Because of this, and other complications, his parents keep a close eye on developmental milestones. One of the most anticipated by my daughter, Lily, was his first smile. There have been a lot of challenges and milestones that we have watched this strong young man reach and overcome. He is a lot like his parents—determined!

So, there it was. The biggest, cheesiest grin I have ever seen. Jackson had finally smiled. Shirley was playing pattycake with him, it is a different version than the one I know, but apparently it works because not only did he smile, but he also laughed! Can you believe it!?!? Every female in the house was cooing and fumbling for cameras. This was a big deal! I did not know what to do since he was not old enough to high-five, so I just sat there stunned. Jackson had smiled.

Another milestone for our children was the first step. It has been a long time since our children learned to walk, but now we get to experience it again through our grandchildren. I have watched animals and all manner of humans take this first step and they are usually quite similar. They stand there for the longest time contemplating the step. You can see the longing in their eyes and the consideration of the possibility of using a different way to get from A to B. Eventually, with great effort, they lift a leg only to topple or just sit back down because it scares them a little to be off balance. I suppose it is a similar process with adults that have been disabled in various ways.

The first step or attempt to take a step usually sets off a chain reaction in parents. From that point forward, hour after hour is dedicated to standing the toddler up, encouraging them vigorously to step, and then mentally rising and falling with every movement the child makes. If parents could only fast forward a few months to when the child will be into everything, they might not be so anxious to get this miniature person mobile.

Spiritually and emotionally, this reminds me of a principle taught by my friend, Dr. Paul Fitzgerald. He encourages people to take the next loving and courageous step. That's it. Just figure out the next best courageous and loving move for you and then take the step. That is what all parents want from their toddlers—not to run a marathon or to high jump onto the couch—just take one step so I can get it on video, please? The unrealistic expectations can come later.

Why don't we take courageous steps? To get the best advice, talk to Dr. Paul Fitzgerald at Heart Connexion Ministries, or better yet, attend a Breakthrough Seminar.

For now, allow me to make some assumptions. First, the reason we do not take the step is because we are not accustomed to it. The toddler does not have the muscle mass to confidently lift their legs yet. Bottom line, this is hard! The next step is hard because we may have not done it before, or we may not have done it in a long time. How many of us need to exercise?

Generally, we avoid starting because we know it is hard in the beginning. Everyone knows it gets easier, but sometimes what we want right now is just to sit back down—crawling is not so bad anyway. To take the step is to start. Then, in a little while (or tomorrow) we take another step. This is how life works!

Second, we do not take the step because there is a possibility of pain if we move forward. The toddler will fall in every way imaginable. They will fall backward into a sitting position. They will fall left. They will fall right. They will fall flat on their face in ways that will make the parents want to call off this exercise. They will teeter and fall, suddenly fall, and repeatedly fall in every way imaginable. But most times, with a little encouragement, they get back up and they keep at it. In adult life there is physical pain, relational pain, emotional pain, and even spiritual pain. Some of this is necessary suffering and some of it is, frankly, because of other people. Someone hurt us. This can be tricky as we do not want to avoid progress because stepping forward is painful, but we also do not want to keep reinjuring ourselves. Maybe the trick is to learn from every crisis, find the lesson in every hurt, and keep leaning into it.

Third, we do not take the next step because we are not living in the present. The thing about most toddlers is that they live in the present. I do not think that they peer into the future or journey back into the past in their little brains. That part of the noggin gets developed later and we adults are very good at imagining ten steps down the road when we really need to focus on the next step right in front of us. Often the next step can provide a better vantage point. When we take the next step, we experience and build confidence. Paralysis of analysis can keep us stuck right where we are and sometimes makes us retreat further. Going too fast may cause a face plant but going too slow can cause us to give up.

Let's take a courageous and loving step today! Here, I'll stand you up. *You can do it, come on! Come on!*

---

## FOR FURTHER THOUGHT

Reflect on the statements below. Don't overthink it, just let it flow. You can analyze it later.

1. What is your next courageous step?

   • What would it be like to take this step?

   • What does it cost you to stay where you are?

   • What are some obstacles that must be overcome?

   • Who are some people or resources that would help you take the step?

   • Consider telling someone else that will support you.

2. What are several words that summarize your thoughts about this chapter or what is a quote you would like to remember?

# WHERE PEACE ABIDES

The first time I visited a Catholic church it was as an observer. I had to get credit in seminary for studying a faith that was different than my own. This was a new experience for me and though I had to gain points for my class I was still curious about it. I started to feel uncomfortable when I missed my chance to genuflect at the end of the aisle. I tried to go back and make up for it, but you can guess how well that went. My next fumble was when the priest invited us to *"greet each other as we always do."*

When the person in front of me said, *"Peace be with you,"* I was supposed to say, *"And also with you."* What I said out of reflex, in a southern drawl, was, *"How ya doin'?"*

Everyone looked at me: "Bless his heart, he's an outsider!"

My current pastor, Brian Zahnd, occasionally answers my messages to him with, "Be at peace." Earlier in life I learned that peace was not the absence of turmoil, but rather it is the presence of God. My spiritual director, Sr. Marcia, offers the traditional, "Peace be with you." I have come to appreciate these sentiments as more than a passing greeting like, "How ya doin'?" What I now hear in these greetings is the lament of Jesus when he mourns over Jerusalem and longs for the people of God to know the ways of peace.

I finally realized what was so satisfying about the visit with my children that night in IHop. We did not cooperatively solve the problems of the world. We did not discover the secret political formula. We did not even agree on every single topic that night. We still have things we disagree about, we still have things that irritate each other, and we still all have our annoying habits that make us snap at each other. What we are all finding individually, though, is peace. Peace is not something we discover corporately or through legislation, peace is something we find individually. This peace changes the world.

So, to close out this series of writings, I offer the following poem which came to me as I approached a milestone in my life. I shared it with my pastor—he told me I am on a good journey.

## WHERE PEACE ABIDES
*by Karl Forehand*

Peace in quiet waters,
Peace in troubled seas,
Peace is hope, Peace is truth,
The truth that sets us free.

Peace in lonely places,
Peace in noisy crowds,
Peace is quiet, Peace is voice,
It speaks my name aloud.

Peace in busy schedules,
Peace in tranquil rest,
Peace is comfort, Peace is power,
The power to strive for best.

Peace in happy friendship,
Peace in angry foes,
Peace is weakness, Peace is strength,
The strength to help us know.

Peace in joyous living,
Peace in painful death,
Peace is living, Peace is dying,
The dying that helps us live.

*Peace be with you!*

---

## FOR FURTHER THOUGHT

Reflect on the statements below. Don't overthink it, just let it flow. You can analyze it later.

1. If I said to you "Peace be with you," what would you think that means?

2. What are some practices that will increase your chance of peace?

3. Meditate on the poem "Where Peace Abides." Does it say anything to you about peace?

4. What are several words that summarize your thoughts about this chapter or what is a quote you would like to remember?

# A NOTE FROM MY WIFE

Over the last few months, while Karl has been working on this book, I could not help but be flooded with memories and emotions. It is somehow bittersweet to see images of my children over the past 28 years flash before my eyes. It feels like it was just yesterday, remembering the bike wrecks and skateboard tricks of our son, Jordan. Images of Abbey and Lily taking a mattress and sliding down the attic stairs only to find out Abbey has a scar to prove that they did not always make it down safely. I learned to pick and choose my battles, but it was not always easy. As a pastor's wife, I constantly felt my children were a direct reflection of me. If they weren't living up to the ideals of whichever church Karl was pastoring, I felt it was somehow my fault. If the church was disappointed, then surely God must be. Not only did this probably cause unnecessary pressure on my children, but it also caused me to form an unrealistic image of God. There is no doubt that God was with me and certainly did change me, but in the day to day grind of motherhood, I did not really pay attention to God softening my heart toward him through my children. Instead, I saw God as someone who daily, if not hourly or minute by minute, required perfect performance from me. And his love was contingent upon that.

On July 18, 2017 my entire world turned upside down. I liken it to a mini-nervous breakdown. You see this was the day our first grandchild, Hollyn, was born. This 5-pound, 8 ounce. little life changed everything about my life. It was when I held her that it was as if God reached down and shattered my heart. Nothing would ever be the same again. As I held her, I knew that the God I knew did not exist. The demanding, retributive, disapproving God that I had known all my life was not there in that moment that I first held Hollyn. As I held her in the hospital, literally hours old, I felt a love like none I'd ever experienced. Do not misunderstand. I love my children and would 100% die for them. This was different, however. There was such a peace—a calm—about this love I had for her in that moment. There was nothing Hollyn did or did not do to earn it. My love for her just "was." I loved her because she was. She simply existed and that was enough. It was as I held her close to my heart that the Divine reached down to mine and whispered "This, my child, is how I have always loved you. You exist and that is enough. You are loved. Lean into my heart as Hollyn leans into yours. Rest and be held."

In February of 2018, our youngest daughter, Lily and her husband went in for what was supposed to be one of the most exciting times in a pregnancy, next to the birth…the day you find out the sex! This, however, turned out to be one of the scariest times in her pregnancy. This is when they learned that Jackson had CMV. I do not want to be the one to tell her story. I just remember absolutely not knowing how or what to pray. The world of ministry taught me that prayer is a must. Not only praying, but it has to be the right words mixed with the right amount of faith. The thing is, I had no clue what the right amount of either was. What if I got the words wrong? If Jackson was not healed, would it be because I did not do something right? Then, on August 8, 2018, Jackson arrived. All 2 pounds, 14 oz. of him. The first time I saw him was not like the first time I saw Hollyn. I could not hold him. He was so very small. He had tubes going everywhere and monitors that beeped constantly. I remember Lily saying, "You can touch him." There is a very specific way you have to touch a preemie. You cannot stroke their skin or rub them because their skin is so sensitive. Instead, you have to "contain" them; literally putting your hand on them with light pressure and just remaining still. As I write this, I feel a lump forming in my throat. I flashback to opening that incubator and putting my hands in to touch him. In those minutes I remember hearing the audible sound of my tears hitting the floor. You would think that prayer would flow in such a moment, but I still had no words for this tiny life. Yet, looking back, I see how in that moment my tears were the perfect prayer and the Divine heard them. He held my hand while I contained Jackson and he held my heart as I cried.

Through my grandchildren, God is deconstructing what I thought I knew. It has been painful. Some days still are. I continue to question how God is showing his/her unending, unconditional love for me through these two small lives. I am learning that I am held. I am learning to sit as the Divine sits, cries, sings, and dances over and through me. I am learning that it is ok not to be ok and that there is value in the scary, dark days. There is also beauty in all of it. But, most importantly, I am learning that not only do I embody Divine love, truth, and wisdom to Hollyn and Jackson, but they reflect such things of the Divine to me. And I am forever changed.

—Laura Forehand
February 6, 2019

# A NOTE FROM MY SON

While my childhood home is in Nebraska, my current home is in Taiwan. I am uncertain on how I can contribute to dad's book, I read it in two days.

These are my thoughts as I sit in a hotel room in Japan away from home today:

I love my dad. I know that sounds trite, but it is true. He is a great guy and has been my role model from before I can remember. This is something that a lot of people say, I know, but for me it is true. I am a lot like dad. We like the same sports teams, aside from Oklahoma University (boo), though I do cheer for them when they aren't playing against my Longhorns. We like a lot of the same old music—Johnny Cash for example. I also held the same political and religious beliefs that he did for much of my youth.

Up until high school.

Which coincides with this book quite aptly. As my father stated earlier, he taught my sisters and I to think critically. While I do not think I am particularly intelligent, I do try my best to gauge the veracity of claims and beliefs that I hold. During the last 2 years of high school, this led me to distance myself from the religion I grew up with – the religion of my father who, at the same time, was also a practicing preacher/minister/pastor (or whatever you want to call it).

I'll try not to rehash what my Pops has already gone through, but we certainly came from a place of fundamentalism. He grew up in it and so did we (my sisters and I). However, I feel that I had somewhat of a unique experience.

My first memories are from Omaha, Nebraska. This is not a town particularly known for its progressive values. One of the places I grew up in included a crazy woman who threatened to beat up my then mother who was pregnant. I had many friends of color.

This may seem insignificant to many, but I think for me it sparked something. I do not even remember noticing this, at the time skin color was irrelevant to me. However, as we moved on from Omaha to southeastern Nebraska, then later to northwestern Missouri, it began to give me pause.

All the people suddenly became white. Obviously, this is not a bad thing inherently; I did not consciously register it. I made new friends both when I started elementary school soon after the move to small town Nebraska and after our move across the river to Missouri.

I mostly went with the flow through elementary school and junior high school. I was the good pastor's child—I had to be, everyone knew who I was. I distinctly remember in early elementary school a middle-aged person approached me on the street one day and asked, "How are you JD?"... *Who the #&\*@ is this?* I thought. My reply was always, "I am good, and you?"

When I started high school, I put my dad's critical thinking lessons into action. I had taken his lead on being a mostly good person, treating others as I want to be treated (mostly), doing the work now so I do not have to do it later (I do not always keep that one)—you get the point.

I started thinking for myself and I wondered if it was all BS.

First, I wondered why many of the "good Christians" I knew were blatantly racist (not to mention openly homophobic)? Many of these people were "good friends." Yet, in spite of one's religion, skin color, etc.—"why shouldn't one be free?" especially in the "land of the free?" While I did not fully realize my beliefs until college, or perhaps this exact moment in time, I believe one's ideals should be fluid as time continues. I began to ask questions.

I enjoyed being in church for the most part. I did not like waking up early (I still do not). I like my current job as an English teacher at a cram school in Taiwan—I can sleep a bit later and work in the evening. That being said, I did like running AV for my father's church in Missouri. I was able to sit in the back and watch the theatrics. People on the edge of their seat, people hanging on every word, people sleeping, all while I drank soda and listened to my dad speak the things that were on his heart.

I remember a lot of my dad's jokes and sayings from this time, he still uses many of them. He is a sweet guy who wants the best for everyone, which is why I am glad he's my Pops. I know so many people who have parents that hate each other or hate their parents, sometimes both. I love both of my parents, I know they love me and one another.

My Pops has a desire to make the world better. He wants to get rid of his own "shadow," while striving to help others shrink theirs as well. He does this through many avenues: coaching, speaking, and activism (namely his veganism). I think the biggest reason why he has made such changes over the years is the same reason I did. We both have a willingness to question and augment our ideas based on evidence. If I had to give the most important lesson that I think my parents taught us, I think it would be this: Question everything.

This is likely why my parents, siblings, and I get along so well. Sure, we have arguments (sometimes at high decibels), but we always love each other in the end. We eventually listen and find where we are on the same page and agree to disagree where we do not. Sometimes we even change our mind to agree with the other person's points (unheard of, I know). This can be seen in our development in our beliefs both political and spiritual.

I will not linger on my political beliefs (if you want to hear about those you can check out Free China Post or Free China Pod), My faith, like my father's, has greatly shifted. As he mentioned we all have a bit of a bad taste in our mouths regarding organized religion, or maybe better stated, fundamentalism.

We have all been moving on through this process for a number of years and I think that this is one place where every member of our family is in a different position, but it seems to be ok for all of us. We discuss it and share our stories to help each other consider ideas that may help us grow. I personally have spent more time in Buddhist, Taoist, and most recently, Zen temples than churches in the past few years. Therefore, I think the most powerful chapter in this book, for me, is about our trip to the tea shop.

Talking about Christian minutia and dogmatism hasn't excited me for a long time. Since late in my college years, when I worked for a Taiwanese woman (a great person and clearly not a Christian), I began to question the idea of God only as the white Jesus I had grown up with. This woman is one of the sweetest people I have ever met. I worked for her for over four years and she has always treated me like family, invited me to family dinners, and I am attending her son's wedding this month.

To think that this woman would be sent to hell simply because she doesn't believe in white Jesus is something I just cannot stomach. I have personally had moving spiritual experiences in Christian churches, various temples, tea shops, bars, and various other locations. It can be listening to a concert or having a deep, life changing conversation in a night market. Just the other day I had a conversation in a random restaurant in Japan about the history of Judaism, Christianity, hell, and much more. This is my church, this is my community.

Some people need a church. Some need a temple. For others there's a need for something else. Or maybe all of the above. What I do know for sure is that we all need to distance ourselves from fear, from fundamentalism, from hate.

So I find that as I sit in this hotel room in Japan, away from my home in Taiwan, what I do know is that what I have experienced, how the author of this book (my Pops) experienced, what we need more of in our world is people asking questions and critically evaluating the answers they hear with the facts on the ground.

We need to keep questioning and finding God(s) wherever we find it/them.

—J.D.

# ENDNOTES

## FOREWORD

1. John1, MSG

2. John O'Donohue, *Walking in Wonder* (Dublin, Ireland: Veritas Publications, 2015), Print.

## WHAT GOD IS LIKE

1. Hebrews 1:3, NIV

2. Matthew 5:44; Luke 6:26; Luke 6:35

3. Matthew 5:39; Luke 6:29; Lamentations 3:30

4. Luke 23:34

## THE LOVE OF GOD

1. Ted Dekker, *The Forgotten Way* (Outlaw Studios; 2nd Edition., 2015).

## GOD IS IN CONTROL?

1. Isaiah 41:10

## RELIGION AND PRACTICE

1. William Paul Young, *Lies We Believe About God* (New York: Atria Books, 2017).

## CELEBRATING

1. John McMurray, *A Spiritual Evolution* (Open Table Press, 2018).

2. Baxter Krueger, *Across all Worlds: Jesus Inside Our Darkness* (Regent College Publishing, 2007).

## THE TEA SHOP

1. Bob Goff, *Love Does* (Thomas Nelson, 2012).

## TRIBALISM, NATIONALISM, AND EMPIRE

1. Brené Brown, *Braving the Wilderness: The Quest for True Belonging and the Courage to Stand Alone*, (Random House, 2017).

2. 1 Peter 2:9, Gal 3:28, Colissians 3:11

## VIOLENCE AND WAR

1. Luke 10:29

## THE PERILS OF FEAR

1. Bertrand Russell, *Why I am not a Christian*, Lecture, 1927.

2. Will Smith, "Will Smith on Skydiving – Fear," YouTube video, 6:05. Posted May 2017. https://youtu.be/VsTBCQ2MnRM.

For more information about Karl Forehand
or to contact him for speaking engagements,
please visit *www.KarlsCoaching.com*

 **QUOIR**

**Many voices. One message.**

Quoir is a boutique publisher
with a singular message: *Christ is all.*
Venture beyond your boundaries to discover Christ
in ways you never thought possible.

For more information, please visit
*www.quoir.com*